Pathologies

Pathologies

A LIFE IN ESSAYS

Susan Olding

FREEHAND BOOKS
an imprint of Broadview Press

Library and Archives Canada Cataloguing in Publication

Olding, Susan
    Pathologies : essays / Susan Olding.

Includes bibliographical references.
ISBN 978-1-55111-930-4

    1. Olding, Susan.   2. Authors, Canadian (English)—21st century—Biography.   3. Teachers—Canada—Biography.   I. Title.

PS8629.L45Z53 2008   C814'.6   C2008-903539-9

Freehand Books
412—815 1st St. SW
Calgary, Alberta
Canada T2P 1N3
www.freehand-books.com

Book orders
Broadview Press Inc.
280 Perry Street, Unit 5
Peterborough, Ontario
Canada K9J 7H5
phone: 705-743-8990
fax: 705-743-8353
customerservice@broadviewpress.com
www.broadviewpress.com

Printed in Canada using 100% post consumer waste paper, certified Eco-logo and processed chlorine free.

Freehand Books, an imprint of Broadview Press Inc., acknowledges the financial support for its publishing program provided by the Government of Canada through the Book Publishing Industry Development Program (BPIDP).

For my parents

Contents

pathology:

1. a. The science or study of disease; that depart-
      ment of medical science, or of physiology,
      which treats of the causes and nature of
      diseases, or abnormal bodily affections or
      conditions.
   b. *transf.* The sum of pathological processes or
      conditions.
   c. The study of morbid or abnormal mental or
      moral conditions. Also in extended use.

2. The study of the passions or emotions.

—The Oxford English Dictionary, Second Edition

Pathology

I'M ALONE IN THE APARTMENT, hunched over the computer screen, writing. The phone rings, and I shrug, as if to dislodge a fly. Let the machine do the work. But when my mother's voice comes echoing from the speaker, I groan and stop typing. Better to talk to her now than later. Better to get it over with.

So we talk. About the weather, about her sisters, about her neighbours—light, safe topics we've discussed again and again. Suddenly, she changes the subject. "Do you get up to go pee in the night?"

"Yes," I tell her, startled into honesty.

"I thought so," she says. "You're exactly like your father."

"Oh, come on." I suppress a sigh. "What's that supposed to mean?"

"Just what it says." Her tone is dark, decisive. As far as she's concerned the conversation is over. "You're like him," she insists. "You are."

My father is a pathologist. The origin of the word contains clues to our riddled relationship. *Pathos*, meaning pity, desolation, suffering. *Logos*, meaning reason. The word.

Once, when I was fifteen, I asked him to describe his work. My friends had started to wonder what he did for a living. "Tell them a pathologist is a guy who uses big words and pisses in the sink," he said.

In simple terms, pathology is the scientific study of the way things go wrong.

We live about 300 kilometres apart. Frequent trips used to bring him close to my city, and once he held a five-month contract in a hospital less than an hour away. Yet during an eight-year period my father visited me just three times, and I could go six months without seeing or speaking to him.

When I was three or four years old, my parents asked me which one of them I loved best. "I love you both," I said.

My mother looked at my father. She was smiling. "We won't be angry," she claimed. "Everybody loves somebody more than anybody else. It's natural."

The June sun slanted through the west-facing kitchen window, staining the pine cupboards golden. My father was pouring cocktails. Light sparked off the bottles into my eyes as I shifted from one foot to the other, considering the question. My mother often yelled at me; sometimes I hated her so much it scared me. Yet she was there, she was present; whereas my father, handsome and interesting as he might be, was hardly ever around. Still, I hesitated.

"I love you differently," I said.

"Come on. Don't be so cagey."

My finger traced the countertop's speckled surface. I had a habit of making up stories about the people I saw scattered in its irregular blotches. Sometimes I told those stories to my mother as she stood ironing or peeling vegetables; sometimes she answered with stories of her own.

"Mum," I finally blurted. "I guess I love Mum the best."

I will never forget the look on my father's face, the way it buckled and broke as he picked up his glass and congratulated me for my honesty.

Failure of adaptation as seen in pathology may take one of two forms. It may be a simple inability to respond adequately..

It is a dark Sunday afternoon in November. I am four or five years old—I have not yet learned to read—and I am sitting on the green couch in our basement family room. My mother holds a novel; my father is watching the football game. No one has spoken to me for a long time.

"Mum. Dad. There's nothing to do. What can I do? What can I play with?"

"Shh. Susie. We're busy."

"But Mum. I don't have anything to do."

"Don't be silly," my mother says. "You have all kinds of things to do. You could play with your dolls. You could draw something." She glances at my father who is frowning and leaning towards the set.

4

"I've been drawing for hours and I don't want to play with my dolls. It's no fun on my own."

"Quiet," my father says. His jaw twitches. "I don't want to miss this play."

"Why do I always have to be quiet? It's not fair."

"Susan. I'm warning you."

"But I mean it. *Why?*"

"If you don't shut up right now, I'm going to give you a spanking. Do you understand?"

"But everybody else has something to do."

"Christ Almighty, you're stubborn!" My father leaps out of his chair, looms above me. As he raises his hand, I cower into the cushions of the couch.

Our dog is lying in front of the fireplace on the floor between us. Fleecy is a miniature poodle, smaller than regulation size due to something my mother describes as a "hole in his heart." With women his disposition is exuberantly flirtatious; men he regards with varying degrees of apprehension and animosity. Now, as my father's hand descends towards my bottom, Fleecy's suspicious black eyes track the motion, and in the split second before the hand strikes its target, he vaults forward and sinks his sharp, smelly teeth into my father's own behind.

"Jesus Christ! Goddamn you, you goddamn dog!" My father wheels around, yanks Fleecy out from under the couch where he's already vanished, picks him up by the scruff of the neck and holds him overhead, shaking him until the white curls quiver. "I'll teach you to do that again, you goddamn animal!" he is shouting.

"Jack, no!" my mother shrieks.

"Daddy, don't hurt him! I promise I'll be good."

But my father doesn't even stop to look at us. Instead he gives the dog a final shake and flings him with all his strength to the floor.

For a minute or so, the only sound comes from the TV where the announcer calls an out of bounds. At last my mother begins to cry. My father stands there, his breathing laboured, his arms dangling heavy and awkward at his sides. Then, gradually, his face seems to rearrange itself, the anger draining away and a look of confusion replacing it. From my seat in the corner of the couch I observe this transformation. Cautiously uncurling myself, I crawl towards the inert figure on the floor, flexing my fingers to pet the springy fur.

Still squatting, I lift my hand away and look up into my father's frightened eyes. "It's okay," I whisper. "It's all right. He's still breathing. Everything's going to be fine."

More usually, disease is partly the result of an adaptive mechanism being turned against the host instead of working to his benefit.

He drinks. As a young medical student he hosted illicit late-night poker games on the stainless-steel tables of the darkened lab; he pissed in the sink to reduce his trips through the hallways where the risk of getting caught was greater. He used to love to quote Newton's Third Law of Motion: For every action there is an equal and opposite reaction. Now, for every tumbler of rum, he swallows another of water. This way his sleep is less serene but his hangovers are milder. As far back as my memory extends, evenings at home were punctuated by the sounds of ice cracking against glass, of voices cracking against each other. I can't recall a night when he didn't reach for the bottle. To me, such drinking was ordinary, unremarkable, as habitual and familiar as mealtimes, or prayers, in other households.

Pathology cannot be said to have laws, as thermodynamics has laws, but it does have recurrent themes. The first...is that disease often originates from a perversion of a survival mechanism.

My mother asked my grandmother, my father's mother, whether she had ever regretted having three sons. Had she ever wished for a daughter instead? "If I had to do it again, I'd sooner have three abortions," my grandmother told her.

Once he brought home a human heart. I followed him as he carried it downstairs to the basement bathroom. He rinsed it under the faucet.

"Let me see, let me see!" I stood on tiptoe and peered into the porcelain sink. The heart looked different, somehow, than I'd imagined. Bigger and smaller, both. Hard and soft at the same time, the ventricles like open

eyes. I watched as he dried the thing off, wrapped it in a
plastic bag and an old towel and placed it in a sturdy
cardboard box. He was packing it to send it to Montreal
where the daughter of former neighbours of ours
attended medical school.

"Dad. What was wrong with it? What went wrong?"

"Shh," he said, looping string around the package.
"Put your finger there," he instructed. "I want to get a
good tight knot." He knelt so his eyes were level with
mine, wrapped his fingers round my forearm and gripped
it. His pupils were dark points.

"Don't mention this to anyone, ever," he said. "Don't
you ever tell anyone about this."

When I cut myself, he used to say, "Put pressure on it.
Pressure stops the flow of blood. Put pressure on it."

The second theme is that failures of adaptation tend to be self-
reinforcing and progressive. In other words, once a patholog-
ical process has started "one damn thing leads to another."
This is best seen in long-lasting illness…

I am nine years old. It is late and I am supposed to
be asleep. I am in bed, but the light is on and I am
reading. Nobody notices. My younger brother is
already asleep in the room next to mine. Across the
hall, my mother lies in my parents' darkened bedroom.
After calling out to him at five-minute intervals for
what has seemed to me like hours, she has finally given
up on my father.

He sits downstairs in the living room. I can hear the ice cubes rattling in his glass; I can hear Johnny Cash on the stereo. Occasionally, a match strikes as he tries to relight his cigarette, which keeps going out. At the sound of his footfall on the stairs my hand darts out for the light switch.

"Are you up in there?" he whispers. "Are you up?"

The door creaks. "You are up," he says. "I knew it."

"Don't you think it's time for bed, Dad?"

"Yup. Yup. You're right."

He sighs heavily and sits down on my bed, staring off into the middle distance. "I brought you something." He hands me a piece of cardboard. "It's Valentine's Day. I made you a Valentine."

I take it from him. Using the red cigarette box, he has fashioned a jagged heart shape. The outside says *duMaurier*. Inside, in his messy, left-handed script, the date and both our names appear. He looks at me warily.

"Thanks, Dad," I whisper, my voice gentle and conciliatory. "Thank you." From his expression I understand that I have managed to avert disaster. "Don't you think it's time for bed?"

"Yup." He wiggles his eyebrows, like a dog bewildered by the sudden disappearance of a ball. "Yup. I just wanted to give you that. Okay?"

"Okay."

After he is gone, I fret with the Scotch-tape hinges of the card, wondering what to do with it. In the end I get out of bed and shove it in the left-hand drawer of my desk. The junk drawer. I do not look at it again for many years, but whenever I feel ashamed, in my mind's eye I see a flash of scarlet and the dumb angularity of his writing.

In the hours immediately following his return from work, my father rarely spoke. Trailing the scents of tobacco and formaldehyde, he'd head straight up the stairs to his room where he'd shed his clothes and do what he called his exercises—a brief Tourettic riff of push-ups and sit-ups. After his shower, he'd pour the first drink of the evening, settle into his accustomed chair, and open the newspaper. He sat like that, his face invisible behind the paper fence, until it was time for the second drink. Later, he'd prop a thick medical text or a shiny journal on his knee while he watched television. My mother sat in a corner of the couch across the room with her own glass and her own book. As the hours passed, her voice would grow louder and her comments more outrageous as she struggled to provoke some kind of response from him. He seldom answered her. In these hours, if he spoke at all, it was only to swear at the flickering screen.

I am thirteen years old and I've just entered high school. It's a clear, bright September night and my new best friend comes to meet me after supper. My father greets her at the door. He nods at her mutely, his forehead creasing and uncreasing.

"A beautiful night," he finally says. "Can you believe it. My God. Such a beautiful night." Leaving the door ajar, he steps unsteadily outside and ambles onto the lawn. "Got to cut the grass," he mutters to no one in particular.

"We're going for a walk, Dad."

"What? What?" He lurches toward us. In his hand, the glass tilts, the scent of rum colliding with the smells of grass and trees and flowers.

"I said we're going for a walk."

He stares at his feet and frowns, as if this is too difficult a concept to grasp. "God Bless. God bless you both," he finally answers.

My friend waits until we are out of earshot. "Is your dad always that weird?" she says.

A third theme is that quick bodily responses to unfavourable environmental events are often overdone...

My father taught me how to skate. He bought me hockey skates so I'd be able to lean forward and go fast without any picks to trip me. He taught me how to swim, too, in the ice-cold waters of the Atlantic off the coast of Maine, where I learned to watch for jellyfish and developed respect for the undertow. My mother didn't join us for these sports. She waited inside with a book and a cigarette, a frown knitting her brow.

When I turned eleven, they told me about menstruation. "When it starts," my father told me, "you'll have to be more careful with the boys. No more wrestling, no more horsing around."

"But why?" The answer didn't really matter. After all, I was not in the habit of wrestling.

But when my period came, I figured out what he really meant. When I needed new skates, I got figure skates. He began to go swimming without me.

Suddenly, he was angry with me all the time. Nothing I did met his approval.

I felt the same about him. I ate my meals alone, a book propped in front of my plate. If he came into the room I slouched deeper in my chair, hoping to avoid him, and when he turned his back to pour the rum, I'd stare at him, my accusations loud but unspoken.

Once, when I was sixteen or so, he made fun of something I was reading. Dostoevsky, I think it was—*Crime and Punishment*. "What do you get out of that stuff? You don't really understand that."

"Of course I understand it," I snapped. "What do you think I am, stupid?"

"Oh. She thinks I think she's stupid." He set the bottle down on the counter. "You think you're pretty special, don't you? You think you know it all."

My mother used to say, "Your father loves you. It's just that he has so much stress at work."

Stress? *Stress?* His patients are dead, aren't they?

A fourth theme is that pathological duels...tend to be fought to a draw rather than outright victory. The reason for this is that natural selection favours such a conclusion for both parasite and host...

Three months until my wedding, and I am home to make arrangements with my mother. We sit, together with the man I am marrying, in the bright, disordered kitchen. My father is downstairs, watching the football game. As we're concluding our deliberations about the guest list, he enters the room to pour another drink. My mother turns the conversation to the subject of my dress and he leans against the counter, listening.

All my life I have known that on my wedding day my parents expect me to wear my mother's gown. I have never thought to question this. I've seen the dress in pictures, of course, and once or twice I've even touched it, as my mother, in moments of nostalgia, has occasionally been persuaded to try it on for size. It is satin, with long sleeves and a high collar, no lace, no train, just a tight bodice, a graceful sweep of skirt, and a hundred tiny buttons. A simple dress; a beautiful dress; and although secretly I wonder what it might be like to choose my own gown, on the whole I am looking forward to wearing it.

"You'll have to have it taken up, of course," my mother is saying. "You're a couple of inches shorter than I am."

"Over my dead body," my father croaks.

"What?" The three of us look at him in some confusion.

"Over my dead body, I said. She's not wearing that dress."

"What are you talking about, Jack? Of course she's wearing the dress. It's what we've always planned."

"No. *No.* Never mind what we planned. She's not wearing it."

My boyfriend shifts uncomfortably in his chair.

"Jack."

"I said she's not wearing it. She doesn't deserve to wear it. She goddamn well isn't good enough to wear it and I'm not going to let her get away with it."

"Jack, for Christ's sake, what are you talking about?"

"That's a *white* dress. *She* can't wear a white dress. You could wear it, but she can't, and I'm telling you, I goddamn refuse to let her. And I'm not paying a goddamn cent for this goddamn wedding, either."

"Jack, stop it!"

"I won't stop it, I tell you. She's not wearing that dress. You deserved to wear it, but she's a—"

"Go ahead! Say it. *Say* it," I scream. "But forget about coming to my wedding."

The wedding takes place, as scheduled. My father pays the expenses, and I wear my mother's gown, which in any case is no longer white, but a mellow, glowing ivory. In the chapel's tiny vestibule, I take his arm, realizing, as I do so, that I have not touched him in years.

"Nervous?" he asks. His own hands are shaking.

"No," I lie.

He eyes me gingerly, draws a deep breath. "I'm proud of you, Suz," he mutters as the organ swells above us and we step into the aisle. "I'm proud of you."

It is the first and only time in my life that he addresses those words to me.

Reflection on these themes provides the beginning of a conceptual basis for pathology but still leaves the student with a bewildering variety of diseases. It may be convenient for him to consider these as belonging to one of four broad categories...the classification consists of inflammation, degeneration, and neoplasia, and a fourth group which cuts across the other three, namely congenital or inherited disease...

14

Inflammation: heat, swelling, burning.

Six years later—a dark time in my life. In the space of a few months, I have ended my marriage and dropped out of law school; I have looked for work but been unable to find it. I am lonely, frightened, and broke. My father gives me some money. Every month, for quite a few months, he sends a cheque, enough to cover my rent and a few necessities. He does not ask me questions.

I go home to thank him. The words are hardly past my lips before his eyes grow bright with tears he won't permit himself to shed. "Don't think of it," he says. "I know times are rough. I'm glad I was able to do it."

I ask him how he feels about my decision to leave law school. "Disappointed," he acknowledges. "But you've got to do what you want to do. I always did." He sips his drink. "After all your fooling around in high school, I never thought you'd get in. And the degree is a prestigious one. But that's just for me. You know how it is. When people ask, 'What's your daughter doing?' I can tell them, 'She's in law school.' You shouldn't pay attention to that."

Half an hour later we have moved to another room
and he is describing his recent trip to the Maritimes to
my brother and me. I ask if he stopped to see his own
brothers, both of whom live there, neither of whom he
has seen in years. His pupils contract. "Right," he says.
"Right. And just what would I have said to them when
they asked about my daughter? They show me their
grandchildren, they tell me about their son the lawyer
and their daughter the nurse, and I say what? What? Oh.
Susie. *Susie.* She's quit this and she's quit that and she's
not doing *anything.*"

I sit, stunned and motionless, listening to the ticking
of the clock. Finally my brother begins to talk about
something he heard on the news. But my father interrupts him. Fixing his eyes on mine, he hisses: "I excelled.
I always excelled. You'll never know what that's like
Susie. You'll never excel at anything."

Degeneration: loss, falling away, morbid deterioration

A few years after my divorce, I took the train to visit
my parents. My father came to meet me. For a moment
I didn't recognize him. His hair was whiter and thinner
than I'd remembered; his ears seemed suddenly larger.
He was driving a new, and quite powerful, sports car, and
he had trouble hearing me over the whine of its engine.
When we got to the house I noticed how stiff his walk
had become.

I had planned to stay for two full days. But on the
morning of the second day my father asked if I was ready

to go. He wanted to drive me to the train. It wasn't until my bags were packed and we were on the road that I understood what was happening. Taking me to the station any later in the day would have interfered with the new start of his drinking hours, moved forward, since his retirement, from five or six in the evening to one in the afternoon.

Neoplasia: new growth. Neoplasm: an area of tissue whose growth has outstripped and become independent of the adjoining tissue.

"She'd make a good lawyer, that one," he'd say of me. "She'll beat you in any argument." This was, and was not, a compliment.

No fiction reader himself—I never saw him with a novel—he couldn't understand the lure of made-up worlds, couldn't understand this daughter. What was I doing, with my nose always buried in a book? What was I doing, sitting cross-legged night after night on the green shag carpet of my bedroom, tapping the keys of a child-sized portable Underwood? Sometimes he would open the door to my room and ask me to explain, but I'd snap the book closed without marking my place, yank my stories out of his sight.

"Just who do you think you are," he'd say. "Who do you think you are?"

Congenital: born with. Inherited: from the genetic material of the parents.

I have his high cheekbones, his strong jaw, his square and capable hands. I have his delicate skin, clear and bright and fair, vulnerable to sun, wind, internal storms.

When I was twenty-one, I fell into a deep depression. I lost myself, lost track of everything I knew or thought I knew. I couldn't see a reason to go on; the world became two-dimensional, a cartoon, as I stood outside it watching. It was a time without words, a time cut out of time.

This depression was the first in what proved to be a series. And then, when I was thirty-one, in the pretty light-filled living room of my own apartment, I felt the senseless palpitations, the constricted, broken breathing of my first anxiety attack. No reason for it, no explanation. Just fear, like a bat, settling on my shoulder and making itself at home in my hair.

I did all the right things. I submitted myself to therapy, took up a program of exercise. But the feelings didn't leave me—they just became easier to live with. And even now there are nights when I stare into a bottle's depths as if into the eyes of a friend, nights when I pour myself another glass, and another. And then another.

Like 1. *similar to, resembling something or each other or the original, as the one is so will the other be…*

Not long ago, I spent an afternoon at the medical library of the local university. I wanted to know how an autopsy is done. The word's literal meaning is to see for oneself; to conduct a personal examination. But the definition doesn't tell you how to go about that, or what it might do to a person, to perform the operation day after day, year after year. In the library I discovered a 19th-century abstract called *The Post Mortem*, but I couldn't find a more recent text. I asked my friend Lynn, who's a doctor, to describe what she remembered from medical school.

"Not much," she admitted. "I'm sure there is a protocol, but I've forgotten it. There were rubber boots, plastic buckets to catch the blood. Hoses to wash it down. The tables were made of metal. The room felt cold, really cold." She shivered, recalling the scene.

"First they slashed the back of the head and pulled the scalp over the face, like a flap, so the face was completely covered." She made a motion with her hands, demonstrating. "Then they cut into the skull, horizontally, with a saw—I'll never forget the wailing of that saw—and lifted the top of the head off, as if it were nothing but a cap, leaving the brain exposed. But later, when they finished the examination, they smoothed the scalp back over the skull, and if you didn't know better, you'd never believe they'd been in there. The face was unscathed. I guess the idea is to leave everything looking intact, in case there's an open coffin."

"What else?" I prodded.

"Well...it's different with the body. There, they aren't so particular. Oh, they examine the limbs and take everything apart methodically enough—labelling pieces of this and pieces of that and sending them off for analysis—but when it comes time to put it together, they just stuff the organs back into the cavity any which way at all; they don't bother putting them in place. Then they take some thick black thread and a fat needle and sew up the hole. It makes a crude scar—no, not a scar, but a *wound*. It can't be a scar, because it never heals, right?" She paused, looking at the floor. "That bothered me, for some reason.

"And another thing bugged me. At the first autopsy I watched, the resident was a young woman. She noticed that the patient had suffered from gallstones. Just before they were about to stitch him back together, she held the gallstones up in the air—as if they were a trophy—and said, 'Would anyone mind if I took these?' And then she took them. She actually *took* them and put them in her pocket. And nobody said a word."

It takes gall to write about the living.

On Saturday mornings the year I turned seven, my father sometimes took me to the lab. The hospital doors snapped open automatically. Inside, men and women wearing white coats glided across floors that shone like the dishes in television ads. My father sat in his windowless office and spoke into a dictaphone while I stared at cells through a microscope. Afterwards, he escorted me to a room across the hall and pointed to the containers lining its many shelves. "What do you suppose this is?" he'd say, indicating one of the jars of tissue, pulling it closer so I could get a better look. "You've seen this one before, you know. We talked about it on your last visit."

Together we peered into the murky liquid. I wrinkled my nose at the smells. Out in the hallway the sounds of another doctor's name crackled over the loudspeaker, and a pneumatic tube wheezed and thumped as someone delivered blood samples from another floor. My father rotated the jar, then rotated it again, so I could see its contents from several different angles; he opened the lid, pulled gently with tweezers, laid the dripping organ on the metal countertop.

"Go ahead, Susie," he said. "Go ahead and tell me what you see. You've had a good look now, a good long look. So name it. Name it."

The Other Country

Dr. Corbeau made me sick.

She flew into the examining room, her dark hair shimmering, her shrewd eyes scanning the scratch marks on my chart, her small hands with their sharp nails riffling through the pages. The mere sight of her made me nervous, but since she was one of the few doctors accepting new patients in the city I'd recently moved to, I couldn't afford to be picky. My jaw tightened at the pitch of her voice, so insistent, so acerbic, so anxious. Ten days ago she had announced that my blood pressure was too high and she was taking me off the pill.

Timidly, I said, "My sex life."

"You should get an IUD," she said.

My jaw dropped. She shrugged and thrust some pamphlets in my hand.

Now I was here for follow-up. From my perch high on the table, I watched her seize the blue rubber pump. *Breathe*, I told myself. *Deep breaths*. She fastened the cuff round my arm, then tightened it. Her narrow wrist was bronzed from a weekend of tennis. *You should wear sunscreen*, I thought. The cold mouth of the stethoscope jolted me. The needle surged.

Her eyes narrowed. "You did stop taking those pills?"

"Of course." My pulse was knocking.

Shaking her head, she pumped again, then dropped the rubber bulb as if it had burned her.

"That's it. Get down. Get out of here. Get to the hospital." Beneath its tan, her face was pale. She scribbled her readings on a sheet of blue paper.

"Do you understand? Get to the hospital *now*. You're going to stroke on me."

Stroke. The word slammed like an iron bar or a steel door between us, blocking thought, blocking all possibility of communication. Stroke. *People die of that*. Stroke. *But I'm not old!* Stroke. *And I'm not ill!*

I was thirty-two, slim, a non-smoker, a moderate drinker, with no history of stroke or heart disease in the immediate family, with no risk factors at all, other than a decade's worth of carefully monitored oral-contraceptive use. Apart from visits to the doctor, I'd never felt better.

Get to the hospital. What can Dr. Corbeau have been thinking? How did she expect me to get there? Was I supposed to drive? I hadn't brought a car. What can *I* have been thinking? Why didn't I call a taxi? But I didn't. Instead, clutching the note she'd given me in sweaty fingers, and with a dazed stupidity that still astonishes me, I walked the two miles to the local emergency room.

A pair of young residents took charge of me. While one drew blood and delivered it to the lab to be screened for possible secondary causes, the other cuffed me again, and asked some questions. "Any unusual headaches? Blurry vision? Dizziness?"

No. No. And no. "Sometimes after my run, if it's really hot outside, I feel a little woozy."

"You *run?*" He frowned. "I don't understand these readings. Right now...the pressure's a bit higher than normal...but nothing like the figure your doctor quoted. I'm going to leave you for half an hour and see what happens." When he returned, he shrugged at me. "It's gone down. Borderline, I'd say. Go back to Dr. Corbeau in a couple of days. She may suggest medication."

Ordinarily we think of illness and disease as identical and use the words interchangeably, but historically, philosophers have found it helpful to distinguish between the concepts. "Illness" most often refers to an individual's experience of suffering; "disease" refers to the theory used to explain the illness, to define its presumed causes, and to describe the paths it will take.

Not ill, I had said to myself in Dr. Corbeau's examining room. Nor was I, if "illness" equals suffering. Still, I left the hospital stamped with a new label and a new identity. *Hypertensive.* Hypertension is a disease, a chronic and potentially threatening condition. In pamphlets issued by the Heart and Stroke Foundation, it is called a "silent killer." I imagine it as a bird of prey, a raptor.

Since that June afternoon, my blood pressure has fluctuated, mostly within the normal range, but even at its lowest, it is higher than average, and visits to the doctor send it soaring. "White Coat Syndrome," this is called. Researchers disagree about its significance, but surely such sensitivity suggests pathology of some description. Should I salt my food less, refuse that extra glass of wine? Should I be taking medication? The questions hover, unspoken, but never beyond awareness. More accurately than many of us, I can predict my ultimate end. The insult to the brain, the sudden affront to the heart. I *feel* just fine, but thrombosis always shadows me.

Before modern technology, a "disease" such as hypertension, unaccompanied by "illness," was literally unthinkable. But suffering without explanation, "illness" without "disease," has long been with us. About a year ago, I received an overdue letter from a friend. She apologized for being such a poor correspondent; she'd had some health problems; she hoped I'd understand. The trouble began with a strange ache in her breast while she was nursing her second daughter. At first she feared cancer, but a series of tests had ruled out that diagnosis. Meanwhile, the pain spread, first to her arms, and then her legs. Her doctors began to investigate for multiple sclerosis or another disease of the central nervous system. But that trail also ended in a blank wall.

Some days, my friend can't type; she is a lawyer, so she finds this inconvenient. Some days she cannot tie her daughters' shoes; she is the mother of two toddlers, and so the ache in her heart competes with the ache in her fingers. Her pain is real, and really debilitating, but she doesn't *look* unwell, and she is growing tired of the doubt she reads in people's eyes. Now her doctors are talking about a virus, or fibromyalgia, or depression. Especially depression. "They think it's all in my head," she says. "Yes, I'm depressed. *Of course* I'm depressed. They'd be depressed, too, if they hurt all the time and nobody believed them!"

Chronic conditions threaten the well, and undiagnosed chronic conditions, like my friend's, threaten the well most profoundly. Chronic conditions defeat sympathy: *Get over it, already!* Chronic conditions invite blame: *It's just her personality.* Chronic conditions challenge the reigning, and therefore comfortable, conception of disease as ontological—a separate being, an invader coming from outside and capable of defeat. Chronic conditions are not so much something we "have" as something we "are."

Or something we become. My friend's undiagnosed disease, her inexplicable illness, is a constantly hovering presence. She has worse days, and better days, but even at her best, she is never as she once was. Still, that doesn't imply she is *less.* The neurologist Oliver Sacks writes about his patients' "creative adaptations" to their problems—the ways they "reach out to life—not only despite their conditions, but often because of them, and even with their aid." We are all familiar with the more mundane examples: the myopic child, no good at sports, who becomes an avid reader; the uncle whose heart condition persuades him to walk, and whose walks awaken the amateur ornithologist in him. Suffering may not ennoble, but inevitably it changes our perspective.

Sometimes it releases us to become more fully our-selves. "There is, let us confess it (and illness is the great confessional), a childish outspokenness in illness; things are said, truths blurted out, which the cautious respectability of health conceals." So said Virginia Woolf, who knew illness more intimately than most; intimately enough to recognize its attractions as well as its drawbacks. Chief among those attractions, for her, were the enforced idleness and solitude of the sickbed. Illness gives us a rare opportunity to set responsibility aside, to indulge ourselves with clean sheets and hot tea and flat ginger ale, to release ourselves from the burden of always doing and always being present to others. "In health the genial pretense must be kept up...In illness this make-believe ceases...We cease to be soldiers in the army of the upright; we become deserters."

Deserters—and loners. An aunt of mine, following a brave and ultimately successful battle with breast cancer, remarked to me that although her family's love and support had been important to her throughout her ordeal, she had come to see her struggle as a journey that must be undergone alone. At most she might share parts of it with other survivors. No one who had not "been there" could offer much in the way of aid; no one who had not "been there" could fully understand.

Illness is another country. Its borders are often unmarked. We can't always tell when we're crossing, but once we're on the other side, we have only to breathe the air to know we're no longer at home. Meanwhile, our doctors in their bright white coats stand guard, dispensing pills like bits of bread to guide us back, their machines anxiously shrieking the alarm whenever one of us slips past.

Dropping the blood-pressure gauge in her office that day, Dr. Corbeau had stared at me as if I might be dangerous. Hypertension is not infectious, of course—and if it were, I'm convinced that the contagion must have spread in the opposite direction. But Dr. Corbeau wasn't taking chances. *How dare you*, her expression said—as if I had demanded dual citizenship of unfriendly neighbouring states, states requiring sole and mutually exclusive allegiance. Behind her indignation I read fear. "You're going to stroke on *me*." Leaving her responsible. No wonder she was anxious. But there was more. "*You're* going to stroke on me." I—a woman of comparable age, class, appearance, education—not old, nor poor, nor fat, nor ignorant—was going to stroke on her. The army of disease was encroaching, too close for safety or for comfort.

She needn't have worried. The diseased don't think of the well that way. They don't want to take them over, or take them along. They don't want to go themselves. Walking from her office to the hospital, wondering if that walk would be my last, wondering if I'd have a chance to say goodbye to the people I loved, it was the light I noticed most. Hard and glinting on the main street, filtered and green on the side roads leading to the lake. The breeze, pungent with the smell of someone's newly painted shutters, rustled the leaves of the maple trees and bent the blades of grass. Swallows swooped and chittered in Edwardian gingerbread. Some children sailed past on bicycles, calling out to one another. My pulse—surely too fast, too loud?—set up an answering cry.

Not long ago, I fell sick with the flu. I lay for days in my bed, memorizing the shapes of clouds outside the window, memorizing the pattern of stitching on the quilt. I could not work. I could not think. I could not eat. My sense of time collapsed—the hours dragged, interminable, or else they galloped, and the day disappeared before I knew it had begun.

One morning, I woke at dawn to the clamour of crows. Raucous, insistent, clanging, their alarm went on and on. Our yard was deep and thickly treed; in addition to birds, it was home to mice and skunks and racoons, but to these the crows were ordinarily indifferent. Healthy, I would have been actively curious about the cause of their distress; ill, I was no more than dully aware. My ears, already thrumming from infection, hardly registered the insult. I tried to read, I swallowed Aspirin, I dozed.

In the afternoon, my neighbour called. "I know you're sick, but I thought you might like to know. There's a Great Horned Owl in your spruce tree."

"So that's what's been bothering the birds."

"Go and take a look at him."

I bundled myself in a sweater and went outside.

The crows had given up; the yard was silent except for the crunch of twigs beneath my feet. I squinted through eyes swollen and crusted with conjunctivitis. The owl perched in magnificent imperturbability midway up the tree. His feathers—golden, brown, and gray—glowed in the weak winter sun. He watched me coolly as I circled the ground beneath him, his body entirely still, his big head swivelling in its socket, his amber eyes unblinking. Such conservation of energy, such concentration of power! In less than a second, he might have left his perch and clamped his talons into me, or any other creature moving through the garden. But he did not—not this time. Instead, at fall of dark he flew, his great wings throwing shadows across the roofs and the parks and the roadways of our city, mapping his mysterious path, back to the country he came from.

On Separation

I know a recipe for almond cake. It's simple—only six ingredients. It can be mixed in a single bowl without any fancy equipment. Made with a touch of lemon, no butter and next to no flour, it tastes light, grainy, and delicious; the experience of eating it is a bit like biting into a cloud. But I shy away from baking it. To make this cake, you need to separate eight eggs. And I mean separate them perfectly, not letting a single drop of cadmium yolk—not even half a drop—spill into the pool of frothy whites. Those whites are all that give the cake its loft, and if you spoil them, you have to start over. Separating eggs is a finicky, sticky, delicate job. The kind I avoid because it scares me.

Separation 1. *the act of dividing or disconnecting*

Jennifer, my sister-in-law and friend, discovered the lump in her breast when she was taking a bath. She was thirty-two years old, brimming with the plans and plots of youth—contemplating a new career, planning a trip to Singapore, conspiring with me about how to get my home-loving brother to join her, and sure, *almost* one hundred per cent sure, that she felt good about their decision not to have children.

She found the lump and went to visit her doctor. The doctor examined it and said it was nothing. Absolutely nothing. And so, over the next year, when the lump didn't disappear but seemed to move and to grow, Jennifer remembered those words and reassured herself. Her new business was up and running, and she was running with it: a massage therapist, she took her table to her clients rather than the other way around. *Mobility Massage*. Dissatisfied with simply treating people and then vanishing, she designed and developed a newsletter to keep her clients informed about new developments in alternative health care. She was busy. So busy. How easy it was to put aside any niggling questions about her own health. Especially since her doctor had said she was fine. Especially because she had never felt better. But her fingers, trained in touch, had knowledge of their own. Inside her body, cells were dividing, then multiplying and multiplying again. Later, after the surgery that was supposed to cut the cancer cleanly out, she told me, "I knew. A part of me knew. But I didn't want to know. It's as if I just pushed that part of myself away."

A tool exists for separating eggs. It looks a bit like a tea strainer, but instead of a mesh basket its bottom is a metal tray with slots around the sides. You break the egg over the separator, and the yolk slides down to the centre, while the white slithers through the slots into the bowl you have placed—or should have placed—

below it. Manufacturers of this device claim that it makes the job quick, easy, and antiseptic.

Quick, easy, and antiseptic—the way I'd imagined my own parting from my parents when, at twenty, I left home, exchanging a messy suburban bedroom with green shag carpeting for a bachelor apartment within a concrete-and-glass box in the centre of the city. The sparkling surface of its windows belied the roach-infested cupboards of the place, but when I loaded my few belongings in a van and drove away I didn't know that. My mother helped me pack. From overstuffed drawers she pulled and kept pulling kitchen gadgets that I barely knew the names of. Potato masher. Jar opener. Grapefruit sectioner. Egg coddler and egg separator. What would I do with these things? With all the steely superiority of youth I watched her hands tremble as she wrapped them. I felt relieved to be making such a clean, decisive getaway.

A few months later, we were talking on the phone. She told me she'd been sleeping so much better since I'd gone. "Now that you're out of the house, I don't lie awake waiting for you to come home at night." She sounded almost cheerful. Outside in the street a siren blared. From down the hall came a hollow thump as someone closed the garbage disposal. I was lonely, but I couldn't have named the feeling, any more than I could have named those kitchen gadgets now wedged in the backs of my drawers. "I have to go now," I said. "I'm working tonight." Afterwards, on the bus to the restaurant where I waited tables, it occurred to me that she hadn't even asked when I planned to visit.

2. coming apart [syn: break-up, detachment]

Around the time of her diagnosis, Jennifer cut her hair, trading her long, straight, light-brown and girlish style for a spiky, gelled and obviously dyed blonde look. It suited her. Forthright, assertive, some might even say tactless—she'd have made a great reporter. Anyone looking to stereotype cancer sufferers as meek, unassuming victims would run into a serious exception in Jen. This new hairstyle of hers advertised her spirit and vitality; it dared her disease to do its worst. And for weeks into her first chemo treatments it looked as if she might hang on to this glorious corona. But then in the shower one morning, her hair detached itself in huge clumps. Some fell to the shower floor and clogged the drain; some she held in her hands. She stared at them for a long moment, then took a deep breath, dried herself off, and asked my brother to help her shave her head. No point in pretending.

Jennifer always chose the direct route if she saw it, but that didn't mean she never got lost. Throughout those first months of her treatment, her feelings spiralled. Skeptical of conventional medicine, she researched everything, and got herself so tangled in concerns about the possible side effects of the different medications she'd been prescribed that it sometimes seemed as if she'd lost sight of the disease they were intended to cure. Nausea, hair loss, lethargy, pain in the arm, bone loss, infertility—is any of that worse than probable death? I had to bite my tongue sometimes, listening to her. She argued with her doctors, challenged them, demanded proofs of safety and efficacy that they could seldom offer.

33

She hated her first support group, comprised entirely of worn-out women in their sixties, seemingly resigned to their fate. The social worker called her "Janice" and told her she needed to do less intellectualising and get in touch with her feelings. "I'll be monitoring to determine if you could benefit from a psychiatric assessment for depressive tendencies," she said. She encouraged Jen, along with the other women, to attend one of those "Look Good, Feel Good" seminars where representatives from various cosmetic companies smear powders and rouges on participants' faces and then pass around a mirror, expecting them to beam with gratitude at the result. Then they bring the wigs out. At this session, the wigs stayed humped in the centre of the table like the Thanksgiving turkey while everyone attempted to look elsewhere, pretending they weren't there. Nobody wanted to try one on. Trying one on would mean removing one's hat and showing a patchy, wispy scalp to all the others. "Oh, what the hell," Jen finally blurted, grabbing the wig closest to her from the pile. They were uniformly awful—tight grey pincurls and Dallas blondes—never designed for a woman of Jennifer's age. "I'm not depressed," she told the social worker later. "And my name's not Janice, either."

She was too attached to life to let it go at the first sharp crack.

Some people use a needle. They insert its point into one end of the egg, making a hole that can then be enlarged by moving the needle slowly in a circular direction. When the hole is big enough, the white will drain out, leaving the unbroken yolk inside. The advantage of this method is its ease. But it can take a long time for the white to drain, and germs from the shell may contaminate it.

A friend and I once disagreed; I've forgotten the subject of our quarrel, but at the time it was important to us both. For a month we exchanged heated, yet considered, e-mails on this subject. In the meantime, we continued confiding in one another about all the other pains and pleasures in our lives, and eventually, it seemed we had resolved our problem. There came a time when she even said she was glad we'd been able to disagree so pointedly and yet remain friends; there came a time when I told her that I'd come closer to her way of looking at things.

Yet I think in those first conversations I must have wounded her, because shortly after that she began to drift away. The comfort and freedom we had known together disappeared, so gradually that at first I barely recognised it. To this day, I don't know if I hurt her; when I asked her if I had done something to upset her, she denied it. Yet something has changed and we're no longer close. How many friendships end that way, I wonder? The sly jab, the slow leeching away. A prick, so swift we scarcely feel it at first, followed by diminishment.

3. *the state of lacking unity*

Jen's illness seemed to change her by making her more fully and completely who she was—though I'm suspicious of saying that, because it seems to give too much power and credit to her disease, when the truth is, maturity would have done the same for her. But because she got sick so young, her illness became her path to that maturity. She'd always been determined; living with cancer made her stubborn. Her strong jaw seemed to precede her as she marched into the specialists' offices. She'd always been organised and analytical and thirsty for learning; now her shelves housed a library of books about physiology, toxicology, and nutrition, and her vocabulary multiplied faster than her traitor cells. She'd go to my parents' house, corner my father, and pepper him with questions. Soon, he'd pull out his reading glasses and the pair of them would sit for an hour bent over his massive medical texts—her head vivid with the hat of the day, his white except for the pink places where his scalp showed through. While my mother made green tea Jen harangued my dad with her theories, most of which he thought were crazy. But he listened. Patiently, methodically, without a trace of condescension, he answered every question. Jen, for her part, continued to look for solutions, in spite of what she read in my father's eyes.

And she tried to live well. She travelled—something she'd always dreamed of, but had always denied herself, out of a fear that she couldn't afford it, or a secret belief that she didn't deserve to do what she wanted. Now she did what she wanted, and watched the world with eyes newly schooled in compassion and wonder. She saw details that once she might have missed: the unshod feet of a construction crew in Bali, the emerald flicker of a dragonfly's wing later that day, at tea.

As she grew sicker—and more truly herself—the people who truly mattered to her stuck close to her. She leaned on friends who made her laugh or who laughed with her. But some failed to recognise the person she was becoming, talked to her only of their own small concerns, did not confront her illness head-on, and from these, she broke away. At first she felt betrayed by their seeming refusal to acknowledge the depth and profundity of what was happening to her. But later, she let the anger go. "I don't have time to worry about it," she told me. She had lost weight, and her translucent skin clung to her bones like a tent to its poles. "If they can't see who I am, why bother?"

Like oil and water, we say sometimes, about a couple who are splitting up. They never should have been together. Like water off a duck's back, we say, watching someone shrug off something of no importance.

By now, Jennifer looked for honesty in others. Could they acknowledge her? Could they acknowledge her losses? Could they look past her swollen belly and her swollen feet and her fatigue and her bad hair and see her burning eyes and still treat her as a person, not a victim? That was her test. And some people failed it.

You can also try a funnel. A small one is best. Place it over a container, break the egg, and watch the white spiral down through the narrow tube while the yolk remains behind.

A funnel's shape contains a swirling vortex. It starts wide, then narrows, like the explanations we sometimes give when we're leaving our lovers. "We just weren't suited," we say to our acquaintances. "We were growing apart." But in private our bland platitudes give way to accusations more specific and less rational. "The way she looked at me with those pathetic cow eyes. I couldn't breathe." "If I heard that braying laugh again I thought I'd die."

4. *the distance between things: "fragile items require separation and cushioning."*

First, the breast. Then, metastases to the sternum and the spine. Then, the liver. Jen's disease progressed and, for all her suspicion of conventional medicine, she forged ahead with the treatments. Surgery, radiation, chemo, more radiation, more surgery, more chemo, more chemo, more chemo. She had always hated and feared needles, so when her doctors proposed the second round of drugs, she drew a deep breath and had a shunt inserted. Supposedly, this would allow her to take her medications intravenously. But the shunt became infected, and then it got infected again. Her GP's failure to diagnose was only the first and most blatant in what became a series of medical mistakes amounting almost to malpractise. Jen's hyper-vigilance began to seem only rational—though sadly, it could not protect her. Her hair fell out a second time. A few weeks after she learned that she had liver metastases, her father was hospitalised with heart failure and died. Her cat got sick. My brother hurt his back. Their washer broke down, flooding their apartment and necessitating the replacement of all their floors. The dryer spun its last cycle and conked out.

We lived several hours apart by car or train and communicated mostly through phone and e-mail. Sometimes, I neglected to make the call I'd been meaning to make. Sometimes I called, got the answering machine, promised to call back—and then didn't. I had my own problems, after all. My own small disasters and victories. My own life.

Like eggs, we sometimes need a little cushioning.

It's possible to buy fresh egg whites already separated from the yolks and prepackaged in sterile plastic containers. You can pick them up in the grocery store or order them online. According to the information on one company's website, egg whites are one of the purest sources of protein, so besides professional chefs and caterers, they market their product to bodybuilders, personal trainers, "Hollywood elites," and adherents of the diet called "The Zone." Their customers put these egg whites into "power shakes" and slurp up muscle-building protein without the fat and cholesterol of the yolk.

I guess I could send away for these packaged egg whites and try them, but somehow I'd feel guilty. A bit like one of those people who trades in her old, stale partner for a lighter, fresher one. It all seems a little too easy.

5. *the social act of separating or parting company*

Many of our most important partings are marked only after the fact. The divorce decree. The funeral or memorial service and the death certificate. No wonder we struggle to separate with grace.

When I first knew her, Jennifer shied away from cameras, consenting only grudgingly to photos. In most, she clowned around. But in the last years of her life she took many self-portraits, serious as well as silly. It was as if she knew that we'd need to see her, to remember her, and that we would need to remember her to let her go. These unselfconscious photos are her gift to us. On my bulletin board at home I've pinned one of her and my brother, taken right after she shaved her head for the first time. It turned out that underneath that spiky haircut Jen hid a skull that was as smooth and perfect as an egg. My brother's broad hand, resting on top of it with splayed fingers, looks like a broken shell.

The last time I visited her, Jen and I sat cross-legged on her bed, holding hands. She had recently developed a passion for Leonard Cohen and in the background I could hear him, weary and ironic, singing about the future. Candles flickered. Her skin shone white in the dark room. Beside her was a glass of water with a straw in it; by now, she could swallow only in the smallest sips. All that day she had eaten nothing but a cupful of fresh raspberries. She told me about the purple light she had woken to the previous night. "Purple, I swear it. This steady, glowing light." She gestured to the window.

"What does purple symbolize," I said. "Royalty? Creativity?"

Never one to prevaricate, she answered, "Death."

We said the things we needed to say to one another. My brother, who had been puttering around in the kitchen, joined us, bringing Jen a fruit popsicle. She gave it a few experimental licks, but couldn't finish it. Before her illness she'd have eaten three of the things at one go.

We sat and talked some more. Then it was time for us to try to sleep. "I still want to visit you in Vancouver," she told me. I was moving there at the end of the week. Jen had always loved the gnarled tree trunks and vivid greens of the west.

"I still want to see you there," I said.

Both of us knew it would never happen. Yet somehow, knowing it, still we managed to hope.

Cleave, that strange word, that means both "to separate" and "to adhere to."

The traditional method is to crack an egg over a bowl, and then to pass its contents back and forth from one half of the shell to the other. If all goes well, the white should drip into the bowl below, leaving the yolk intact. If all does not go well, a ragged edge on the shell will puncture the yolk and the yolk will escape and you will have to begin the process all over again.

Back and forth, back and forth—the pattern of vacillation. I have indulged in it, all one summer, in fact—the summer that ended my first marriage. My husband was devoted. We loved each other. But we had married young and somehow, after only a few years, we found ourselves unable to speak to one another about the things that mattered most. We both felt smothered and guilty—but he would never have said so. It was up to me to make the break. And so I did. He begged me not to go, and part of me wanted to stay. We'd seemed so good

41

for one another, at first. I had hoped to grow old with him. So I kept extending a hand, and then I kept with-drawing it. The pain was terrible, and by summer's end both of us were a mess, broken and stained.

6. *sorting one thing from others*

After Jennifer died, my brother was sorting through some of their things. In the closet he came across a small knitted hat, meant for a baby. One by one he called to mind her friends. None of them had a child that size. Finally, he decided that she had intended it as a Christ-mas gift for our cousin's daughter. Jen died in August. She must have bought the hat months earlier.

In the hospital on the way to her final ultrasound, the elevator broke down. Suspended mid-air, halfway to nowhere, Jen and my brother held one another.

For days after her death, her voice still echoed on their answering machine.

Both names still appear on my brother's home e-mail address.

Her neurotic, despotic cat is his companion. Together, they pad around the apartment, still bright with her presence. My brother drinks his coffee looking out at once-shared views.

For my part, I might be slicing onions or separating eggs and suddenly I'll be shedding tears that have nothing to do with the fumes I'm inhaling or a spot of broken yolk.

The basic and best and bravest way to separate an egg is in your hand. Crack the egg over a bowl, slide it onto your palm, and slowly open your fingers. The white will drip away, leaving the yolk, trembling and solitary and yellow.

7. *the space where a division or parting occurs* 43

Jennifer chose cremation. Her ashes were stored in a compact but surprisingly heavy box. It squatted unopened on the table in my brother's apartment for several days, attended by the various objects we were collecting to take to her memorial service. We bustled around the apartment, making phone calls, writing notes, drinking coffee and tea and beer and composing obituaries and eulogies. Anything to keep busy. Meanwhile, her cat skulked under the bed and sniffed at the tall, almost elegant stand—christened Jeeves—that had held Jen's hydration bags, and the short, efficient oxygen tank my brother had called R2-D2. When at last we peeked into the box, we saw that all that was left of Jen had been stuffed inside a plastic bag.

"You'd think they could do better than that for the price," my brother said.

He and her brothers and her mother decided to spread her ashes over the lake. Her dad's remains were also there and they knew she had loved the place. So after the speeches and the harp and flute music and the tears and the laughter at the memorial service, her closest friends and family decamped to a small and secluded park where my brother, Jen's brothers, and her oldest friend launched a canoe into the water and paddled slowly out.

The rest of us stood on the shore. Some of us climbed down the rocky cliff to get closer to the water. The sun set, staining the sky purple and orange and gold and red—all the colours that Jennifer had loved best. Releasing balloons into the still air, we watched them sail slowly, slowly away and out of sight. A family of ducks came by, rowdily investigating.

On shore, I read the text my brother had asked me to read—a passage from Thich Nhat Hanh. In the boat, Jen's brother read the same words. Then they opened the box of ashes, placed some in their palms, and allowed them to slide through their fingers. Later, my brother told me that the lake was so clear, he could see them for a long time, first skimming the surface like water bugs, then drawn down, and down again, suspended in the water like particles of dust in air.

Purple Hearts

Shannon O'Brien is the quietest girl in eighth grade. "Speak up," the teachers are always telling her, but kindly, because Shannon is well-behaved, precise, and punctual with her work. A good student. A nice girl, or so they believe.

Shannon has not grown into her looks yet. Her thick dark-blonde hair lies flat on either side of its centre part, the way it is supposed to, but the style does not flatter her nose. The popular kids ignore her. She is more popular than I am, though. I am scrawny on top and wider on the bottom. My own dark-blonde hair clumps around my ears in a nondescript half-grown-out pixie cut. I wear black-framed octagonal glasses. Behind their bottle-thick lenses my eyes shrink to watery dots. My arms strain beneath stacks of books, and when the other kids snicker at me, as they often do, I console myself with the thought of what my heroes would say about them.

Shannon and I are in the same math group. One late September day, after ensuring that the teacher's back is turned, she asks me in her sweetest, most musical voice to come out to the back field at recess.

Our school is blessed with an exceptionally large playground. Technically, the back field does not belong to us, but since the nearest development has bypassed it, we older kids claim it as our own. To get there, we have to cross a creek, which in spring flickers with tadpoles, and in summer and fall grows lush with marshy grasses.

My heart thumps. I know no good can come of this.

"What's going on?"

She flushes. "Nothing. We have something for you, that's all."

"We" turns out to mean almost all the girls in our class. Only the most popular—Kim McEwan, Heather Johnson—and the least popular—Cari Dimme—are absent. I watch the girls trot across the wooden footbridge. Head down, I follow. When I was young, a troll lived under this bridge. Gone now, of course, but I still hear the hoofbeats of billy goats.

This part of town is largely populated by Italians whose impressive gardens spill past the confines of their carefully constructed fences. Any trailing or crawling vine roots easily in the rich and fertile loam. In springtime, peas, and strawberries. Cucumbers and zucchini, later on. Nobody bothers to harvest them. Here, on the school's side of the fence, they spread in profusion, bruised, thick as my thighs, and spongy now with rot.

From back in the main yard come the shouts of the little kids skipping rope and shooting marbles. Some boys from our grade are hitting balls over at the baseball diamond. I stare at the girls, lined up against the fence, their hands clasped in mock-innocence behind their backs, their eyes shifting, their mouths trembling with held-back giggles. Cucumber, zucchini, tomatoes. Even the odd pumpkin. My skin prickles and burns.

Shannon is in charge of this operation. She inspects the troops, making sure they're properly assembled and well-stocked with ammunition. She picks up the biggest zucchini she can find. Its underside is mushy, crawling with slugs.

47

"Ready. Aim. Fire!" she commands.

Towards the end of that school year, I host a sleepover, and surprise myself by inviting Shannon. She surprises me even more by coming. We play Twister, grinding chips and dill-pickle dip into the family-room carpet. One by one, the other girls fall asleep. Crickets scritch in the basement a floor below us. Shannon and I move our sleeping bags closer together. By morning we know all each other's secrets.

"Do you think I should grow my hair out?" I ask.

"Definitely. It will hide your ears. They stick out too much."

They do?

Walking home from school the next week, she takes me aside and invites me to be her best friend. The apple trees in the surrounding yards are blossoming, and their scent makes me light-headed and optimistic. "Sure," I answer.

Her green eyes narrow. "If you want to be best friends with me, you can't be good friends with Cari."

For two years, Cari Dimme has been my constant companion. Slow-moving Cari, at whom our teachers are always barking, "Step lively." She has frizzy black hair, a bulbous nose, and small blue eyes behind glasses purposely identical to mine. She has shoes just like mine, too. Also, a jacket. And a binder. And a pencil case. Cari copies me in everything.

But she's loyal. Cari wasn't in that lineup firing cucumbers at me. Besides, she knows more than just my secrets. Cari has practised kissing with me.

"I could be *friends* with both of you, just not *good* friends, right?"

"No. No way. It's her or me."

I can't believe my ears. Is this Shannon talking?

"But why?"

Shannon flushes. Her lips disappear. "Because." She starts to walk. "That's just how it is, that's all." Her hair bounces against her shoulders. The houses look on indifferently. A breeze knocks at the trees, sending pink petals spinning to the ground. I imagine the years ahead, day after day of clomping off to the high school with Cari at my side—Cari, who nods at all my sentences and never has an idea of her own.

"Okay," I shout. "Okay, okay!"

At the village drugstore, Shannon and I buy grape ice cream. It does not taste like grapes, or like any other fruit. It tastes like saccharine wax. But taste is not its attraction. What draws us is its colour, Shannon's favourite—a livid violet. Shannon's bedroom, furnished in teak, is decorated with a purple bedspread, purple curtains, and mauve walls. For our eighth-grade graduation party, I wear a purple granny gown with dotted Swiss sleeves, while she sports a purple hot-pants outfit and purple polish on her long, strong fingernails. We favour Schaeffer fountain pens, which we buy at the drugstore and fill with purple cartridges. We write our names again and again, this way and that, coupling them with boys' names, festooning them with purple flowers and purple hearts.

Shannon is in love with Todd Robinson. I am in love with Steve Andropolous, only I call him Steven, the name he went by back in fifth grade when I first fell for him. Steven's eyes are brook-brown and his skin is golden. His hair crests in a chestnut wave across his noble forehead. He has the straightest, finest, most godlike nose I will ever see. I loved him all through our fierce competition for second place in the fifth-grade class; loved him through his sixth-grade rock-collecting phase; loved him through his seventh-grade crush on that snob, Brenda Billings; loved him through his eighth-grade spin-the-bottle craze for Karen McEwan; and I will keep on loving him until eleventh grade, when I finally get a real boyfriend of my own. Or that's when I will *claim* to have stopped loving him. The truth is, I will love him at least until I am twenty. Maybe I will love him until I die.

Steven Andropolous doesn't know I exist. Or if he does know, he is too polite to say so.

Todd Robinson, on the other hand, is perfectly aware of Shannon's existence. Along with his squirrelly friend, Jeremy Fenester, he comes every day to the schoolyard to check up on her. Shannon and I perch in the gnarled crotch of an apple tree. The Munchie Tree, we call it, after our habit of gnawing on its green and wormy fruit. These apples—or the grape ice cream—give Shannon regular stomach aches, but she persists in eating both.

50 Todd is tall, dark-haired, blue-eyed, and pimple-complected. He wears jeans and a white T-shirt and smokes Players unfiltered cigarettes, storing the pack in his rolled-up sleeve. A year from now we will dismiss him as a greaser and turn away from him when he speaks to us in the halls at school. But for now we find him entertaining. He tosses rotten apples at Shannon, purposely missing her. He wants to go off someplace with her and leave me with that gerbil, Jeremy. Luckily for me, though, Shannon clings to her apple branch. She giggles, but she does not climb down.

When the boys finally give up, we dive to the ground and mount our bikes, careening like bats in the semi-darkness. My bike is a sturdy blue CCM whose serviceable handlebars my father, under protest, has replaced with the fashionable, dangerous, butterfly kind.

"It's National Swear Day," I announce.

"Darn," Shannon says. She says it quietly, the way she says everything. She rides a brand new purple three-speed with hand brakes and a purple banana seat. "Dink."

"Hell," I say, much louder.

"Shhh! Sue!" She blushes.

"Asshole." "Piss." "Shit." "Damn."

We repeat each word a dozen times. We don't know any others.

A year and a half later, we have read my parents' copy of *Fanny Hill*, stolen from the top shelf and never replaced. We walk to the park halfway between our houses and duck beneath the bleachers. Shannon pulls a pack of Rothmans from her pocket and strikes a match. The flame gutters, then flares. We inhale deeply.

"Fuck." I peer through the wooden slats at a tall figure approaching. "Here comes Tony Lukits." Tony lives across the street from the park. Our new friend, Elke, has caught his eye. Elke—full-breasted, long-legged, narrow-hipped in faded Lee jeans. Elke, whose silver-brown shag falls in lustrous waves to the top of thick-lashed blue eyes as honest as I am envious. One day when Elke, Shannon and I were out on our bikes, we passed three labourers. They stopped their work and leaned on their shovels, watching us pass. "I'll take the first one," the tallest, most handsome one said, referring, of course, to Elke. "I'll take the one in the middle," said the second. He squinted, the better to appreciate Shannon's assets, and nodded at his own good taste. The third man spat and shook his head. "Nobody want the third one."

"Elke's not here," I say to Tony.

"Doesn't matter," he lies. "My parents are out. Why don't you two come over for a drink?"

Shannon shrugs. "Why not?"

At the end of Tony's street lies a pine forest, or something that we call a forest. Really, it is a clump of trees left standing to disguise the sewage plant. All our lives we have been ordered to stay away from there, and all our lives we have disobeyed. This year, by some mysterious agreement, half the kids in our school decide to go there for an impromptu party the morning before our Christmas vacation starts.

I volunteer to bring the vodka. It is easy for me to steal it; my parents will never know the difference. "I've got a jar," I tell Shannon, over the phone. "I'll take about four inches. You bring juice."

She brings Tang instead of real juice, and her container is baby-food sized, while mine is an enormous pickling jar. We mix the contents and swallow, gagging. All around us, our classmates huddle, raw-knuckled without gloves, their teeth chattering and their feet inside their Adidas damp from the snow. A popular boy from the eleventh grade notices us and ambles over.

"Don't give him any! What will he think?" Shannon hisses.

But it's too late.

He lowers the jar from chapped lips, his eyes wide. "Not bad. But where's the orange juice?" He draws a sleeve across his face. "Hey—Brad! Come over here. Taste this!"

By the time we get to school, our limbs feel warm and rubbery. If we close our eyes even for a second, the world tilts, then spins. Hundreds of other kids roam the halls in a similar condition. "Can I use your comb?" a messy-looking cheerleader pleads. "Are you going to Myers' party tonight?" "Whooeee! Merry Christmas!" Teachers shake their heads and throw their hands in the air; depending on age and temperament, they laugh or slam doors in disgust.

Elke and I are in the same geography class. Every few seconds her chest convulses and she lets out a croak "I've got the hiccups," she says.

"Hold your breath."

She puffs out her cheeks and convulses again "Doesn't work."

"Then go and get some water."

She wobbles to the fountain. I hear a giggle, then a shout, then silence. She doesn't return. Disappointed, I turn back toward my desk. Just as I am about to take my seat, Blair Robbins yanks it out from under me and I go sprawling across the floor.

"Oops." I stand up and wipe the dust from my jeans "That didn't even hurt."

Shannon stands in the doorway making eyes at me.

"Did you see what just happened?" I shriek.

"I think I'm going to be sick." She leans against the wall, clutching her concave belly.

"Oh, for God's sake," says Mr. Kirkwood. "Get out of here, will you? How am I supposed to run a class? Go, go Both of you! Out!"

Since I befriended Elke first, I am surprised when Shannon goes along with it. Sure enough, after a month or two, she pulls me aside one afternoon to complain about Elke's faults. Elke, it seems, is too much. She has a rubbery smile, a silly laugh, a double-jointed stumble. Mr. Murchie, the drama teacher, calls her a natural comedienne, but to Shannon, she is an embarrassment. She can only be our friend if she agrees to keep herself in line, if she agrees to act more *normal*.

Shannon proposes a formal meeting to establish the terms of this treaty. We hold it at my place. With my bedroom window open, we are free to smoke, undetected or unremarked on by my parents. Elke slumps in the corner of my bed, her shaggy hair curtaining her eyes. I've never noticed it until now, but her chin is hilly with pimples. Whiteheads, blackheads, and drumlins, like the ones we study in geography, except hers are red.

Shannon leads the charge. "You can't always be laughing like that."

"Like what?" Elke protests. "How else am I supposed to laugh?"

"Don't be an idiot. You know what I mean."

"Yeah," I echo, uncertainly. I myself have no idea what Shannon means. Elke is the kindest, most decent, most gentle person I have ever known, and here I am, acting cruel to her. What is the matter with me?

From downstairs comes the sound of my mother, banging pots. It's almost suppertime, and the girls will have to go soon. I light three cigarettes and pass theirs over. We exhale gloomily. Elke makes a fan with her science notebook and waves it around to dispel the smoke. Shannon examines her nails.

"Just try not to stand out so much."

Elke nods. She draws her knees up to her chest and the luscious breasts disappear from sight.

"I like your hair," I say to her. "Would I look okay with a cut like that?"

Tony Lukits is an expert strategist. He recognizes at once that if he wants to get close to Elke, he'll need to create a diversion. He marshals some friends for the mission. Shannon is dispatched to Dave. Dave is tall and lanky, with a sleepy voice and a haircut just like Elke's. He already has a girlfriend. Her name is Denny, and she is plump, squidgy-faced, and almost as quiet-spoken as Shannon herself.

Tony takes us to Dave's place late one night. Dave and Denny are necking in the corner. The television is tuned to a Buffalo station featuring blue movies. On the screen, a woman in fishnet stockings grapples with a man. Elke snorts nervously. Shannon glares at her. The woman moans. Dave disentangles his head from its nest in Denny's hair. The man undoes his belt and pushes the woman onto a bed. Dave's hand, on Denny's back, stops moving.

Shannon stands up. "What *is* this stuff?"

Her body blocks the screen. She is willow-waisted, smooth-hipped. Her long, silver nails flash against blue-jeaned thighs. The pants are literally shrink-wrapped to her body—she puts them on while they're wet and lets them dry on her, to get that look. Dave raises an eyebrow.

Shannon tosses her hair and turns to Elke and me, nestled together on the couch. Her cheeks are pink. "Come on, you two. Let's get out of here."

A week later, Dave dumps Denny.

Kevin is assigned to me. Kevin's pale hair, white frat jacket, rapidly blinking eyes, weak chin, and big nose lend him the appearance of a laboratory rat. In his favour is the fact that his father owns a car dealership, so he drives a slick, forest-green MGB. He is not my boyfriend. He does not come to my house when my parents are home. He does not ask me to the dances. He does not hang around my locker at school. But weekend nights, he comes to the park and asks if I want to go driving with him.

56

I wear my favourite outfit—bedraggled bell bottoms and a tight, white sweater vest appliquéd with a red satin apple. The apple has had a bite taken out of it. This vest was the subject of a bitter quarrel between Shannon and me. Unaccountably, I won, which explains why I am wearing the vest and she is not. But Kevin couldn't care less what I am wearing. He angles his big nose and French kisses me. His damp hand inches its way up my back, blindly searching for my bra hook.

The car smells of leather and oil and the herbal shampoo Kevin uses. Nobody I've ever known is as car-proud as he is; there isn't an inch of this thing that he hasn't scrubbed and polished and dusted and waxed. It looks like a showroom model. The only sign of its true age is the rubber casing around the stick shift which appears to have dried out and is cracking. As Kevin's hand creeps relentlessly up toward my right breast, I stretch out my left arm and pick at this hump of rubber.

He undoes the buttons on my blouse.

Pick, pick.

The windows fog.

Pick, pick.

He tugs at my vest.

I roll the bits of rubber like snot between my sweaty fingers.

He reaches for my zipper.

I squirm and push his hand away.

Wrenching himself toward the driver's side, Kevin stares, appalled, at what my left hand has been doing.

"Shit, will you look at that?"

I shrug.

"Arrgh!" He takes my glasses from the dashboard and fits them round my ears, adjusting them against my nose. Kevin is not such a bad guy. In a year, he'll be dating the girl he will eventually marry. Together with his brothers he will build the car dealership into a solid and highly respected business. My father will be proud to buy his cars there.

"Come on," he says. "Let's get some air."

But it is January. The wind off the lake is cold, and as usual, neither of us is wearing a scarf or a hat. We drive over to Dave's place, instead.

Dave and Shannon are necking in one dark corner. Elke and Tony are necking in another. It is not clear what else they may be doing. Nor will I learn anything later, because, for all our eagerness to find boyfriends, Elke, Shannon, and I are completely silent on the subject of what happens when we are alone with them. Fear of exposure strikes us dumb. We know it is our job to hold the line; that much is clear. But where is that line? Why is it always shifting? How far is too far? How much is too much?

The television flickers. Irv Weinstein and the Buffalo Evening News. On the screen, young men in combat camouflage and white bandages disembark from military planes. They stare straight at the camera—whether in defiance, despair, shock, or wonder, it is difficult to judge. The war in Vietnam is over. The troops are coming home. They have earned their Purple Hearts.

58 Kevin is history. I've been picked. Picked by somebody with thick blonde hair, high, wide cheekbones, and sleepy blue eyes. In the bathroom, the other girls regard me with new respect. "How did you get him?" Hal is one of the most popular boys in the school. He is a funny, dopey, weak-willed liar—almost enough to make me forget Steve Andropolous. He calls me up every night. He takes me to his house to meet his mother. He invites me to the formal and buys me a yellow corsage. He says I have a million-dollar smile. But I should have known it was too good to be true. Even a million dollars isn't enough to keep him when Shannon is around.

What happens? She goes out with his homely best friend for a month. We double date. Next thing I know, Hal is telling me he thinks we ought to stop seeing each other for a while. I pretend it doesn't matter. I avoid the cafeteria at lunch. I stay away from parties they are invited to.

In less than two months, Shannon breaks up with him.

"I knew it. He got on your nerves, right?"

"Yeah," she agrees. "Besides, he kisses weird."

He does?

This is the year we roller skate. It's Hal's idea; he is an expert skater, and because Hal suggests it, the rest of us go along, playing ironically at "Happy Days." Except for Shannon. She sits on the sidelines. "Roller skating is stupid," she says, exhaling smoke through her nose. If pressed by one of the boys, she will claim to have sprained an ankle. I know better. The truth is, she is afraid to fall on her face. Sensing my advantage, for once I decide to ignore her disapproval. I challenge Hal to a race. The next week he invites me for a couples' skate. Our friends exchange knowing glances. I pretend innocence. He doesn't have to pretend.

59

One night, he bets me $5 that I can't stop smoking for two months. For close to two years, I have been smoking a pack a day, so this represents a genuine trial. I succeed, more or less, allowing for the usual cheating at parties. I go to collect my prize.

"I did it," I tell him.

"You want a medal or a chest to pin it on?"

From behind his back he draws a wooden plaque. A crisp new bill has been encased in a kind of clear lacquer called "Preserve Forever." Three weeks later, school starts, and he asks me to the first dance.

That year, I don't see much of Shannon or of Elke. They've got boyfriends, too, but from a different crowd. Hal plays football; their boyfriends are on the same hockey team, Shannon's is another Dave; Dave Two. I call him. Like her first Dave, he is tall and skinny, but unlike Dave One, he has a scraggly line of hair above his lip, and a permanent pout. I have no idea what Shannon sees in him. Elke's boyfriend is called Rick. He is bowlegged, wiry, and altogether too self-confident for comfort.

One morning I am woken at five by the sound of small stones hitting the screen. "Sue. Sue. It's me."

I pull back the curtains and am greeted by the sight of Elke standing on our lawn, skinny-legged as the robins. She looks awful. Mascara streaks her cheeks, her skin is mottled, and her bony knee winks through a hole in her jeans.

"What's going on?"

"It's Rick." She starts to cry.

I let her in, pour her a glass of milk, and ask her to tell me the story. It turns out Rick has been sleeping with somebody else. The worst of it is that everybody else has known about this for months and months.

"You didn't suspect anything?"

"No! Why would I? I don't know where he gets the time. He's almost always with me!" She swallows some milk and sets the glass on the table. "You know what makes me crazy? *Shannon* knew. Shannon knew and she never told me."

I shake my head. My parents are moving around. We can hear the water running through the pipes. Soon my mother will call me to get up for school.

"Mind if I smoke?" Elke opens the window another notch.

I count to ten, watching her, and then give up. "Can I have a drag?"

The illicit hit of nicotine goes straight to my head.

"I like your hair. How would I look, with a cut like that?"

On a hot June afternoon the phone rings. It is Shannon. Dave Two has gone for a family outing and she has some free time on her hands. How would I like to go for grape ice cream?

I weigh this. Shannon never calls except when Dave Two is busy. We don't even walk to school together any more; Dave Two drives her, in Kevin's old MGB. She and Dave Two act like an old married couple. They do their homework, eat supper at one another's houses, watch TV, go to his hockey games and practises, Dave Two pouting all the while. Just the thought of it puts me to sleep. Still, unlike me, Shannon doesn't have to worry about Dave going off on long, mysterious trips with his friends, the way Hal does. Dave doesn't smoke too much pot, or get into car accidents when he's been drinking, or hang out in strip clubs when he isn't with me, or play dumb practical jokes, like Hal. Hal is still operating under the delusion that these are the best days of our lives, and he ought to make the most of them. Dave Two has probably never even thought about it.

Two years from now, Shannon will call me, and say, so woodenly I do not recognize her voice, that Dave has broken up with her. Dave the Dull will have left her for his best friend's girlfriend. Shannon will lose fifteen pounds in three weeks. Her skin will turn gray, her eyes will turn red, her gorgeous fingernails will chip and break. She will stop smiling, speak more quietly than ever, and wake up in the mornings panicked and choking.

But all that is in the future.

The drugstore doesn't carry grape ice cream any more.

"No call for it," the clerk says. Shannon and I roll our eyes. What is the world coming to, without purple ice cream? We pick from among the other flavours, fishing in the linty pockets of our cutoffs for the right change.

Leaving the store, I notice a wire display of paperbacks. While Shannon compares nail polish brands, I examine the covers. One book in particular catches my eye—a white background, with black and gold letters. *Launched a social revolution! Hundreds of thousands of copies sold*, it says on the back. *The Feminine Mystique.* I've heard of that.

I take it up to the cash.

"You and your books," says Shannon.

The Munchie Tree has been pruned back. Even in full leaf, it looks denuded and scarred. We climb it anyway and look out over the playground, reminiscing. High school will be over soon. Neither of us has a firm plan. Shannon might take a course in dental hygiene. Or maybe she'll go to the community college and study computer programming. I would like to travel, go to Europe, walk the places where my heroes walked.

Shannon licks her cone, her expression contemplative. "Remember that day in the back field?"

Do I remember? I can still smell the damp September air, can still feel it like a web across my skin. I hear the thwack and thud of the first missiles, falling short and landing at my feet. I see the other girls' eyes, lit with unholy glee, and guilt, and greed for whatever is going to happen.

My heart thumps.

"You didn't scream, or cry, or run away. I thought for sure you'd run, but you just stood there, watching us, taking it all in. I always wondered about that." She finishes her cone and wipes her mouth. "How could you?"

How could I not?

Such Good Girls

Surplus to the system—that's what they call me. The euphemism may comfort its inventor, but what woman likes the implication that she is too much? No matter how you say it, though, there aren't enough jobs. Four days before the school year starts, I still don't know if I'll be teaching.

Just when I've resigned myself to looking for another kind of work, I get the call. "You've been placed," my principal trumpets. Staffing is a complicated chess game. Unlike his other duties, such as meeting with parents or maintaining morale, it is one he excels at. "You're with us again."

I meet him in his spacious office. Tall, white-bearded, imposing, he dominates an enormous oak desk. The vice-principal, leaner and athletic, stands. They offer me coffee. As usual, it is cold and stale.

"Now that we've got you a job, what extracurricular activities are you planning to get involved in?"

"I'll run the Writers' Club."

"Good." They nod.

"And I'm going to help with the debating team."

"Excellent." They pause. The principal tugs his beard. "What else?"

What else? My assignment will be difficult. New teachers typically get the classes no one else wants—kids who will never go on to college or university, kids who will be lucky to graduate or to qualify for any job in today's economy, kids who struggle to read. Kids who are, in another of those eloquent euphemisms, "seriously at risk." However good my intentions, however noble my aims, for most of our hours together I will be shouting myself hoarse and confiscating water pistols—and worse. Evenings, I'll grade papers, phone parents to track down truants, and scramble through files searching for activities to satisfy short attention spans. What does he mean, what else? Aren't two extracurriculars on top of all that enough?

Evidently not.

"What about cheerleading?" he says.

"Cheerleading? No."

They stare. A grim-faced Santa and his unlikely elf. How can I refuse this gift they are delivering?

"I don't know anything about it."

The VP smiles. "You'll learn."

"I haven't done the First Aid course."

"Not a problem."

"But I'm opposed to cheerleading. I don't even like football!" I back up, stumble on the carpet's seam. Coffee sloshes against the side of my cracked mug. "I'm not the right person for this."

The Principal frowns. "We just need someone to go to the games. You won't have to go to all the practices."

The scale feels like ice against her feet. Watching the needle balance itself, she smiles. One pound less than yesterday. Five pounds less than last week. At lunch she buys no-fat yogourt and swallows it slowly, slowly, her spine pulled straight and her stomach sucked in tight as she watches the other girls, the weak ones, scarfing down chips and chocolate. At night, she bakes. Trays of muffins, jarfuls of cookies, rich, dense cakes that she herself never touches. On her skin, the shimmer of fur, like the down on a newborn bird. Size six, size four—all her clothes are loose on her. She bundles them on, in layers. To keep out the terrible cold.

Tryouts take place in the playground of the neighbouring elementary school. Over a hundred girls show up, all shapes, sizes, and degrees of prettiness. Donna Wall, guidance secretary, golf fanatic, and mother to two girls on the team, plants herself midfield and bellows names, checking them off on her clipboard. Our first job is to sort them—junior or senior, novice or expert, big enough for the base of the pyramid or small enough for its top. A few girls hang back on the edges of the crowd, taking stock of the competition, and then slink away before warm-ups begin. But more stay to perform the absurd set of kicks, jumps, and acrobatics we demand of them. Donna and I look on, shading our eyes with tanned hands. I'm surprised at how often and how easily we agree. After all, what do I know about this? I've always hated cheerleaders. Yet here I am, colluding in this strange selection process: That one has energy, this one doesn't smile enough, that one might develop if we gave her a chance, this one was captain of last year's team. And she looks like trouble. Yes. No. Maybe. Yes. No.

Meanwhile, the experienced show off. Small, incredibly slender girls perch on the shoulders or the stiffly outstretched fists of slightly bigger girls. They smile; they unclip and re-clip their ponytails. The scent of their fruit shampoo and the sounds of their nervous laughter float on the late summer breeze.

Asked why they want to join the team, some girls sound vague. "I don't know. I heard the announcement." Others bridle defensively: "It's hard work, you know! You have to be really athletic!" An honest and unguarded few simply shrug and admit that their friends persuaded them to come along.

Just by attending a tryout, a girl signals her desire to belong, to fit, to be approved of by grownups and peers. Cheerleaders are so pretty in their socks and abbreviated skirts. Cheerleaders are so earnest, are such strangers to contemporary irony. Not for them the piercings, the tattoos, the black lipstick, or the disaffected sneer. Cheerleaders are good girls. Such good girls.

Someone else has left her tracks. Footprints checker the toilet seat. Standing on it, you get a view of your thighs, your ass, otherwise impossible to see in the half-height mirror of this narrow bathroom. She does not bother to wipe the dust away. Instead, she bends, scanning the other stalls to see if anyone is there. No time to waste. Someone could come in at any minute.

Kneeling, she spends so much time kneeling it's a wonder she hasn't formed calluses there, or scars, like the ones that speckle the knuckles of her right hand. The concrete wall feels cool to her forehead, cool and damp. She steadies herself, then plunges her fingers down her throat. Everything comes up, everything—each greasy wheel of pepperoni, each prickly gulp of diet Coke. She waits until she sees green—the lime green of new leaves. It is the peel of the Granny Smith she ate first, just for this purpose. So she'd know when there was nothing left inside her. So she'd know she was empty. Empty.

We're the girls from Country High
Our mothers still bake apple pie!
You think it's easy to milk a cow?
Well, listen up! We'll show you how.

Kelsey-Ann, who leads this chant, also wrote it and choreographed its accompanying moves. She captains the senior team and counsels and advises the juniors. Cheerleading is her life. But the hint of self-parody in her rhyme is intentional. Kelsey-Ann is bright, destined for a first-class university. Small, skinny, with a squirrel-like, piquant face, bad skin, and a good brain—if it weren't for cheerleading, nobody would notice her. Instead, she is one of the school's most popular girls.

No one can say she doesn't work for it. At our school, teams meet every day of the week except Friday, when games are held, and twice on Wednesday. Often on weekends, too. Football and other competitive sports get precedence, so the girls practise on the nearby elementary school playground instead of the high school playing field; on rainy days they are forced to use the cafeteria, with its dangerously low ceilings and adamantine floors, rather than the much safer gym, where the boys' teams all work out.

Cheerleading does not do wonders for the average adolescent's character. The year I coach, our team requires new uniforms. Together, we pore over American catalogues. In the States, cheerleading is big business. The girls sigh over the pom-poms, batons, spangles, sequins, megaphones, and other accoutrements deemed unnecessary—and far too expensive—for more modest Canadian budgets.

"Short skirts," they insist. "Tight tops!"

Donna and I roll our eyes. We're thinking of more practical alternatives—elastic waists, baggy shorts, sweats—forgiving clothes that will flatter different body types. The girls will have none of it. Though they cluck their tongues in dismay at those other girls, the ones who starve themselves to stay thin, they nevertheless skip breakfast, religiously refuse that second portion. And if Jane and Shawna will look silly in skimpy skirts—well, that's just too bad. Serves them right, for making such pigs of themselves. They give the team a bad image.

Nor do they want to pay for the uniforms we order. Walking around practice with a slip of paper and a moneybox, I gain new sympathy for Fuller Brush men. The look of boredom and disgust that falls across the faces of these girls is a slammed door. Their veneer of respect for me cracks and chips away—in their hearts they know I was never one of them. Their excuses aren't even creative. "My mom forgot." "I didn't get paid." "I'll have it next week." "Why do we have to pay, anyway? It's not fair!"

Whining is their characteristic pitch. To the rest of the school they look like a whirling red and gold spun-sugar fantasy, but Donna and I see them differently. Not a practice goes by without one clutch of girls refusing to participate, another group pointing fingers and telling tales, and still another group huddling in a corner, claiming illness or emotional trauma.

The seniors are worst. "Come on!" Kelsey-Ann hollers at them. Later, she pleads, "You guys!" The whispers go on, unabated, until she slumps in a corner, admitting defeat. On the advice of a rival coach, Donna buys a large whistle, but even its shriek fails to hold the girls' attention. The only thing uniting them is their hatred of the other schools' teams. "Those hos," they sneer. "Stupid sluts."

People are astonished to hear that I'm supervising the team. "You hate that stuff!" But one friend, a poet, is more accepting and philosophical. I visit her in the city. Over wine and pasta and coffee, she listens to my complaints, extemporizing:

We're the girls from Country High.
Our mothers still bake apple pie.
Our fathers still fuck baby sheep.
At least our mothers get some sleep!

She chooses a serrated knife. Its blade feels cool against her finger, hot and cool against her arm. Her arm—apple-blossom

*white, rivered with blue veins, and etched with the scratches
and scabs from the other times, the scars she hides with long
sleeves, even in the summer. One cut is not enough. The pain
not sharp enough, not deep enough to shock her awake. So she
cuts again, and again, pulling the blade like a saw, deeper each
time, until a jagged tide of blood spills onto the kitchen countertop. She watches, pupils expanding, as the blood pools,
darker, darker. Then she shakes herself and reaches for a dish-
cloth. To wipe away the mess.*

Not everyone can make the cheerleading team. The girls
I teach don't even try. Sabrina, for instance. Day after
day she shuffles into class just before the bell, eyes down-
cast, shoulders hunched, chin angled towards her chest.
Every time I speak to her, she tilts her head away and
stares at the floor. I ask the other teachers about her.
"What do you know about her family life? Who are her
friends? Is she okay?" They shrug. She's passing her
courses, barely—"at the borderline," we like to say—and
she is never, never disruptive. A good girl, as bad girls go.
No one considers her a problem.

Most bad girls aren't as quiet as Sabrina. Some are
boisterous, bawdy, wild. But even as they thumb their
noses at authority, they covertly glance at their nails to
make sure their manicures are intact.

In a special writing class for failing students, I work with
Candy. Her regular teacher tells me she is vulnerable,
"running with a bad crowd," "making poor choices."
When I ask Candy to write about Fridays, she considers
me from beneath thick-pencilled lids.

"Really?"

What Candy likes about Fridays, I discover, is being with her friends and doing all the "bad" things teenagers typically do—smoking cigarettes, drinking, taking drugs, and "doing blackouts."

I think I know what a blackout is. You breathe fast, hyperventilate, hold your breath. Pass out.

"That's right." She grins. "Just for a minute or two."

"Does it hurt? Is it dangerous?"

"Nah," she scoffs. Later, though, she tells me that she's heard it kills brain cells.

I've always thought that blackouts were a prepubescent thrill. I'm surprised that somebody Candy's age—fourteen—would still admit to enjoying them. I ask her if everybody does.

"No. Not everybody. Just some people. My friends."

"Boys, too?"

"Oh no!" She laughs. How could I be so out of it? "Boys never do blackouts."

At this school, at least, blackouts are practised exclusively by girls. Few methods of silencing the self could be more eloquent.

Ninth grade. An unfamiliar walk through an unfamiliar part of town. Unfamiliar halls, lockers, stairwells, bodies, boys. They are bigger than my father. The school is two storeys tall, and around the central foyer is a balcony where the senior boys hang out. From there they get a good view down the gaping blouses of the girls below.

Eighth grade had been the year of the back-field zucchini brigade. I got no invitations to parties, no phone

calls in the evenings or on the weekends. At the graduation party, I hid in the kitchenette with the parent-
chaperones. "Such a nice girl. Such a good girl," they
later told my mother.

I may be nice. I may be good. But I'm not stupid. This 73
new year in a new school offers me my best opportunity
to become somebody else, and I need to do it now, before
my old reputation spreads. My mission is not for the
faint-hearted. I wear dark, hexagonal glasses that disguise my single decent feature and dominate my pale
face. I keep my bangs long to hide the pimples on my
forehead. But I do know how to turn a cartwheel. I
decide to try out for cheerleading.

The new gym is rank with the smell of old sweat.
Running shoes squeak across the vinyl floor. The
teacher, with her marbled thighs and square jaw, orders
us into formation, commands us to shout our names and
birthdates. "Why are gym teachers always fat and ugly,"
Shannon asks. She has agreed to come along for this, but
when we get there, she chickens out. "Sue. You're
embarrassing me," she says, as I belt out the school cheer.

For years, my mother has been telling me to keep my
voice down. This is my chance to yell. But I don't yell
loud enough. Or my cartwheel isn't as good as I imagine.
Or something. I don't even make the first cut.

On the radio, I once heard some prominent women
interviewed about their history as cheerleaders. Some
said they had joined the team for fun, for excitement.
Some said they wanted power. And cheerleaders do have
power. Despite their low priority in the allocation of

practice space, they remain the queens of the school, included on everybody's invitation list, indulged by their teachers and their classmates.

Yet this power does not come without a price. Cheerleading can be understood as a metaphor for the roles that patriarchy assigns to women. Within a patriarchal culture, all women, like cheerleaders, are supposed to stand on the sidelines, to support men and "build up" men's accomplishments, while our own skills go unnoticed and uncelebrated. Within a patriarchal culture, all women, like cheerleaders, are expected to accept our subordinate position both explicitly, through our words and gestures, and implicitly, through our bodies, which are diminished and trivialized even as the men's are exaggerated.

A strange power, that makes us small and relegates us to the margins.

Seventeen storeys in the sky, I look out my window at blinking city lights, blurry now through the tears I cannot stop. I am twenty going on thirty-five, as my mother likes to say, but inside I am twelve—a young twelve—and tonight I might as well be two. There is no one in the world I trust.

I've been fighting with my boyfriend. In this room, in my presence, he flirted with another girl, a friend of my best friend. Angie is tall, slender, dressed in a snake-green, skin-tight dress, her long blonde hair angled over an elegant eyebrow. She used to be a cheerleader, my friend says—and it shows. When Angie speaks, she sucks up all the attention in the room. When Angie moves, she sucks up all the air.

She is gone now. My boyfriend is gone, too, but he left with my insults in his ear. I said cruel things, and meant them, then, but now I am alone. Sitting on my bed, I rock, seeking refuge in the motion. Sobs rattle my frame. Tomorrow I'll find a speckled rash on my puffy face where the salt of my tears has burnt it. As if I were allergic to my own tears; as if I were allergic to myself.

I pick up my left arm, an arm I scarcely recognise. It is winter, and my wrist is pale. I twist it and stare at its underside. Hoping to stifle my sobs, I stuff it in my mouth. But the sobs go on, my frustration peaks, and watching myself, as if from afar, I bite. My teeth are strong and sharp, and the skin on my wrist is fragile. It does not hurt. I do not feel. I bite down, harder and harder. I will bring myself down to size.

What stops me, at last? I don't know. My apartment is one room. I could walk three paces for a knife, a pair of scissors. Instead, I pull back. The skin is torn in two or three spots. The air feels cool on the welts. For a week I will tug at my sleeves to disguise the raw ellipse.

"Borderline" is the name that psychiatrists give to this behaviour. Borderline patients are not popular. Their problems resist treatment. Their problems seem so much their fault. They are so empty and so absent from themselves. So contrary, so confusing, so insecure, so manipulative. Like everyone's worst stereotype of "woman." No wonder, then, that the label is so rarely applied to men.

75

Borderline, sideline, neither here nor there. Borderline, where even the cheerleaders stand.

November. Time for my performance evaluation. The
principal comes to my classes. He doesn't bother to say
hello or goodbye. He sits at the back of the room in
jacket and tie, his big bulk wedged into the small desk.
Expressionless, he types on his laptop throughout the
lessons. I'm nervous and the students are nervous; no
matter how many times I've told them he'll be watching
me, still they worry that he's come to judge them. Each
class he attends is marked by strange mistakes on their
part and on mine. I'm certain I'll get a bad report.

Instead, he gives a glowing commendation, describing
me as an agreeable colleague, a co-operative junior, a
"good sport," a "team player." Having taken on the
cheerleaders, he means.

*Shhh. Not so loud! Hold your stomach in. Don't touch. Keep
your hands to yourself. Look at the mess you've made! Don't
talk with your mouth full. Don't talk back. Are you sure you
want those seconds? Do as you're told. Why? Because I said
so. I've had just about enough of you. I've had it, up to here.*

We are such good girls. We are all of us such good girls.

Walls of Glass

My office walls are made of glass. Gregory is a tall boy whose Crayola-orange hair seems to vibrate under the fluorescent lights. Long before he taps on the door, I can see him awkwardly approaching. He hunches, shoulders almost level with his ears, and frowns, averting his face from everyone else's.

"Hello," he says, bowing and dipping like some strange old-fashioned toy, one of those stiff-necked plastic birds that bobs perpetually for coloured water.

"I know you're busy. But." His lip twitches.

"Come in. Sit down." I brush away crumbs and swallow the last of my milk.

He shrugs, buckling the stripes on his pullover. Then, closing the door behind him, he peers furtively under the desk and into the farthest corner of the tiny, triangular room. Finally he sits on the edge of the moulded plastic chair, releasing his iron-fisted grip on the dark green gym bag he always carries with him. It falls to the floor with a thud. Gregory is not good at sports, so whatever this bag's intended use, it has never, in fact, held athletic equipment. Instead, it contains books—every text for each course he is taking—and also all his binders. Unlike his classmates, Gregory will not leave these in his locker and pick them up during breaks between periods or at lunch time. Lately, he will not go to his locker at all.

"Counsellors are always busy," he observes. "People coming by. People needing help. Yes. I understand." His voice trails off.

Then he clears his throat. "You know, I was wondering. I need to make a few phone calls. Just a few calls." A sly gleam ignites his eyes. "I have an interview. You know. For a job. A government job. I have to call them immediately."

I have been warned to refuse this request. In the past few months, Gregory has been "doing the rounds" of the counsellors, taking over our offices for hours at a time. *Just one more. Just one more!* he'll insist, if interrupted, shielding the phone with his elbows. He has made at least a hundred calls, racked up a huge long distance bill on the school's account. The secretaries in our main office are tired of fielding angry and confused complaints from the various officers in obscure federal and provincial sub-departments who, so far, have been the main recipients of his desperate calls.

"Gregory. I'm sorry, but no. I can't allow you to tie up that line."

It's true. Any minute now, someone else may call—a desperate teacher, a despairing parent, a counsellor from another school, a probation officer. At the same time, as Gregory knows, my excuse is also a lie. I *could* let him use the phone, if I wanted to.

Abruptly, he starts to cry. I stand to close the blinds—
a recent, much-needed addition to the room supplied by
a sympathetic principal—but no sooner have I done so
than he stops.

"It's okay," he says. "I understand. Of course, of course,
you're busy." His skin has flushed a blotchy pink. He
stands as if to leave, but then does not.

"I think my parents are trying to hurt me," he blurts.
"I think they're after me. I found a trail of papers on our
lawn. And then…and then…"

"Yes?"

"They don't want me to pass my courses. There is too
much noise there. You know what I mean? Too noisy."

"Do you have younger brothers and sisters? Is that it?"

"No. It's them. Just them. They're always *talking*. They
wouldn't talk like that if they wanted me to do well.
They wouldn't. It isn't right. It isn't *fair*. I have a lot of
courses—they know that—a *lot* of difficult courses this
term. So it's pretty obvious, isn't it. They want me to
fail." He smirks.

"It sounds as if you're feeling anxious, Gregory. As if
you're under a lot of stress."

"Stress, that's it. I'm stressed. I need to find somewhere else to work, somewhere quiet. Do you know some
place I could go? Could I stay at the school overnight? In
Mr. Ross's room? Or maybe here, instead." He looks
around again, as if considering the best spot on the floor
for a sleeping bag. "In here would be fine. Would the jan-
itors kick me out?"

"Gregory, have you tried talking with your parents?"

"No. *No!* I can't talk with them."

"You know you can't stay here at night." I hope my voice is gentle. "Do you remember what we talked about last week? Have you thought some more about going to see your doctor?"

He is eighteen. Even if they wanted to—and I am not sure they do—his parents could not force him to go. I can't force him. He has to decide this for himself.

But he grabs his bag and lunges towards the door.

"You *could* let me use the phone, you know. You *could* let me use it. It wouldn't really be so hard for you at all. *You* could use somebody's else's office. You *could*." By this time he is shouting, and if the blinds were still open, I know I'd see the curious faces of his peers, smudge-nosed against the pane.

He slams the door behind him. I want to lay my head on the plastic walnut finish of the desk and cry. My office walls are made of glass. When I open my eyes my reflection stares back, a hollow-eyed woman without answers.

For the past two years, I have worked as a counsellor in a secondary school. Officially, my role is to provide academic support for students who struggle with the curriculum, but inevitably one thing bleeds into another, and I regularly hear confessions, break up fights, and dress wounds both psychic and physical.

They are so easily wounded.

He hates me, they say. *Parker hates me, I can tell.*

What makes you think so?

A shrug. *The way he looks at me.*

No. He doesn't hate you. He hasn't even figured out your name. He hardly knows you exist. He's frowning because this year he has thirty-five students in the class and books for twenty-four, because there are not enough desks in the room, because the child in the seat beside yours cannot read. Or maybe because he suffers from indigestion.

Adolescents take everything personally. Their transparent skins show every emotion. A sad thought can bruise a young face like a plum.

It is a mistake to think their problems are all trivial.

Some have never had a home. Their parents are drunk, or absent, or dead. Some have witnessed murders, finessed drug deals, hit people, hurt people, bent under the blows of another person's hand. They carry weapons—knives, and sticks, and razor blades, or cruel words recalled from long ago. They finger them inside their pockets, say them under their breath. Sometimes they want to play show and tell.

Maryanne is lonely. Her family is new here, and she misses her friends and the teachers at her old school. She says she has no one to talk to, no one she can trust. Least of all her parents, who ignore her plummeting grades, ignore her midnight binges, ignore her frightened eyes, insist she is "all right." *There is nothing wrong with our daughter.*

Abby has stopped eating. She dyes her hair green and pierces her body in a lot of places. Her mother accuses her of taking drugs, which she is, and of stealing money and jewellery, which—so far—she isn't. Becky, aged fifteen, is pregnant. Sabrina slashes her arms, Tiffany was raped. Angela's father hit her when she refused to babysit. Stacey has just been diagnosed with cancer.

The boys don't want to talk. They slump in the corner, bounce paper pellets off the walls, crush pop cans in huge fists, stare vacantly at my posters, or ask if they can borrow my pen and then forget to return it. They stretch their legs out and thrust their dirty boots onto the desk. Without confiding anything, they reveal so much.

I have seen adults, the same adults who argue that teachers do not work hard enough, come into the school and cringe. They pull back in fear, surrounded by these giants, their own children. Yet how fragile adolescents are, like moths' or butterflies' wings. Their big bodies, their braying laughs, their sheen of sex: all lies—or, if not lies, then such narrow, partial windows on the truth.

My office is shaped like a triangle. Its walls are made of glass. On one side is the library, called the "Resource Centre" these days, where the loners and the computer geeks go to hide. Gregory used to cower in a carrel there at lunch, next to his sole friend, the two of them bolting their food and pretending to work. That was before the friend transferred to another school.

On my other side, the doors to the athletic department swing open. There, the big, popular boys of the school line the passage with their bats and balls and shoulder pads, with the booming arrogance of their voices. Mornings, lunchtimes, and after the last bell, these halls are packed, almost impenetrable. Some of the younger girls won't walk this way. Sometimes I avoid it myself.

Not Adam, though. Adam is oblivious. When he arrived here in the fall to begin ninth grade, we thought he might be autistic. In classes, he refused to speak. He did not do his work. At lunch, he prowled the building, cleaving to the walls, flapping his feathery white hands, his too-short pants and too-tight T-shirt snapping with static electricity, his thick dark hair falling in a screen across his face.

Adam has lately befriended me. Having finally discovered the library, he could see me in my office from his lunch-hour hiding spot. One day I waved at him and smiled, and he ducked under a shelf, but three days later, after watching me some more, he tiptoed up the ramp and scratched on the glass. Now he eats with me regularly, his French fries wafting vinegar and grease. Whenever another student or a teacher comes to the door, Adam flees. But when we are alone, he talks.

And talks. Psychological tests have confirmed what I had already suspected: although eccentric and probably "on the spectrum," Adam is not, strictly speaking, autistic. His verbal scores on the Weschler scale approach the highest percentile. At age fourteen, he reads at a university level. He also has a photographic memory. He will glance at the dictionary definition of a word, and five days later repeat it—without a single deviation.

Right now, he is interested in theories of personality. His mother is taking a night course in psychology, and Adam has been reading her textbooks.

"Histrionic," he says, waving a fry as he speaks. "A lot of them are histrionic."

He is talking about his classmates.

"Or they're narcissists. They've got Narcissistic Personality Disorder."

"What makes you think so?"

"Dramatic. Always calling attention to themselves. Have to be the centre of attention. You know. Like what's his name, that guy who came here the other day. Bruce."

"Mmm."

"He's anti-social, too. What did he do? I know he's on probation for something."

He takes a sip of coke.

"And the girls. Always playing with their hair. Writing notes. One minute, they're crying their eyes out because some idiot didn't ask them to the dance and the next minute they're giggling or putting on their makeup."

"Histrionic, eh?"

"Well, maybe not *all* of them," he allows. "But they're extroverts, for sure. Real extroverts."

"Not like us."

He rewards me then with a rare smile.

"What would you say about *your* personality type, Adam? What are you?

Tugging on a hank of his recently trimmed hair, he deliberates. "I don't know. Dependent maybe. Dependent with a bit of anti-social thrown in. Nobody's just one thing, right? Or not very many people."

I would have said Asperger's, or schizoid or schizotypal or avoidant, myself, but now that I hear it, his own diagnosis sounds as likely.

"But it's hard to say," he goes on. "Hard to say. I might change some, in the next while. It's difficult to pin a label on yourself. Don't you think?"

I do.

85

At their age, personality is liquid, like hot glass. Becoming adults, we assume shapes, solidify—or shatter.

Three years ago, when I was still a classroom teacher, Gregory worked with me as a tutor. Even then he was rigid and vigilant and stiff; our students called him "Soldier Boy." He prided himself on his reliability. I can still see him—as obsequious as Uriah Heep, as punctual as the Inspector of Schools, racing against the bell, his green gym bag held out stiffly in front of him, an odd, self-satisfied smile on his pale face.

Later, we had a falling out. On Fridays, I had been giving him lifts into town, driving out of my way to take him to McDonald's, where he worked. We had agreed that he should ask me for these rides in advance, and at first he was religious with his requests. Then, he started forgetting. He would show up at my door at three o'clock and stare pointedly at his watch, while distractedly, clumsily, I gathered up my things. *Hurry, hurry,* he would say. *I don't want to be late!* Or he would neglect to ask me at all and simply wait by my car in the dusty lot. Meanwhile, I'd have promised rides to four or five other students or teachers, and there wouldn't be any room. Sometimes I had weekend plans that would prevent me from going into town at all. One day I had to rush to make a dental appointment. "I can only take you to the traffic lights at Princess," I warned him. "I can't take you all the way this time."

Gregory at first agreed, but as we drove, he began to argue about it. His voice took on a hostile tone I'd never heard in him before; he was rude and obstinate and demanding. In retrospect, I see this was a warning sign, a symptom of his breakdown, but at the time I was preoccupied with my own worries and indignant at his ungratefulness. I asked him to put himself in my shoes: would he want to do favours for people who complained and took him for granted?

He was not open to reason. He clenched his jaw and started shouting at me. His pale hands trembled. I pulled over to the curb then and asked him to get out. After that, he avoided me in the halls, looked down when he caught my eye, consumed his library lunches in a carrel more hidden from my office. So when he suddenly appeared at my door again and asked to make his phone calls, I knew he must be desperate. Who could forget humiliation like that, except in direst need?

Summer, and I am walking across the campus of the university. First the new library, with its wide stone plaza, wooden benches, and freshly planted trees; next "Fort Jock," the big athletic centre, surrounded by beds of vivid flowers. Students spill out of doorways, glide by on bicycles, shout to one another from across the street. I am enjoying this walk—the sense of freedom any holiday brings, the feeling of sun on my skin, the beauty of the young, fresh faces all around me.

Suddenly I hear a familiar, yet unplaceable, voice.
Someone is calling. Someone is calling me.

Missus. Missus!

I am not a "Mrs." Nobody calls me that. It must be a former student, one of those sweet, old-fashioned, well-meaning ones who can never get Ms. out of their mouths. I stop and spin around, my sandals scraping the pavement.

Gregory?

I recognize the red hair, which seems to shiver in the sunlight. Otherwise, he is greatly changed. His illness has swollen him. Or perhaps this new puffiness is a side-effect of medication.

Has he started taking medication?

In less than a month, he has gained at least twenty pounds, and his striped pullover, too heavy for today's heat, strains at all its seams. His skin gleams with an unhealthy sweat. His suffering is so palpable, and so incongruous here in the warm sun, among these glowing young bodies and faces, amid the brilliant flowers, that I want to look away. I *do* look away, and then force myself to turn back. His own eyes dart and flicker. He drops the green gym bag on the ground.

"Have you been working out?" I ask, astonished.

"I have, I have," he stammers. "I graduated, you know. Even passed chemistry. I'm taking a couple of courses.

Part-time. My marks aren't good enough for full-time. But they let me use the facilities."

"Congratulations, Gregory. You had a rough term. I'm really glad you made it."

Maybe he will be all right.

"Yes." He sighs, scuffing his shoe against the sidewalk, a smile dawning at the corners of his pale and blistered lips.

Maybe he'll be fine after all.

Then he chuckles. "Well, you know. Got to get in shape. Got to get myself in shape, to take that government job."

It is late. The buses left a long time ago, and all the halls are silent. My office is a triangle. Its walls are made of glass. On one side of me, the library, with its stacks of dusty books, its unremembered poems and unread stories. On the other side, a gym, haunted by the ghosts of athletes past, where the smell of stale sweat permeates the air, even when the room is empty.

My third wall is a doorway. Who is walking through it now?

How to Be a Volunteer

Be punctual.

Arrive on time at the appointed place. A different group will be meeting there. No sign will point you in the right direction; no one you ask will have a clue where you should go. Don't give up. Rely on the sound of a woman's voice to draw you through the dank stone corridors; her confident bark. She is blonde and wears crisp khakis, a blue blouse, and one of those wristwatches that displays the date, time, and current weather conditions of every developed and underdeveloped nation in the world. To see her is to know you have arrived.

Sit with your thighs pasted to a plastic chair through the video presentation. A narrator will intone the Red Cross mission statement while slides of mostly white people distributing food and clothing to mostly brown and black people will flash across the screen. Everyone will be working hard and smiling in these pictures. They will remind you of a UNICEF Christmas card—a circle of stylized children holding hands. A paper doll chain.

Notebook entry
Volunteer: One who voluntarily offers or enrols himself for military service, in contrast to those who are under obligation to do so, or who form part of a regular army or military force.

Conversation with R. She's against the military. She's also against volunteering. Anybody who signs up for either is suspect, as far as she's concerned. In fact, it's not just volunteers she distrusts. Teachers, doctors, nurses, counsellors, social workers, child care workers, shelter workers—all, she says, are exploiters, colonizers, and cannibals of human souls. The only caring relationships she sees as legitimate are family relationships. Mothers are okay. (She's a mother.) Fathers, uncles, aunts—fine. Friends can offer help. But to be committed in any public way to the welfare of others is to signal a secret wish to use or even abuse them.

How about all the abuse that occurs in families? I asked.

That's different, she said. It's not institutionalized. By definition, people in the helping professions feel superior to the people they're helping, a couple of rungs up on the ladder of life. And mostly they're not helping those people, anyway. Mostly they're just helping themselves.

The stone must have bounced off a passing truck, snuck along Fidanete's sock, and crawled inside her shoe. Now it is lodged between the footbed and her sole. With each step it bites her tender flesh. But she does not bend to untie her laces. One glance at her mother, trudging beside her, persuades her not to. A vertical pleat scores the older woman's forehead. A knot compresses her lips. She smoked her last cigarette an hour ago, and there is no telling when she'll get another. Better to leave her to her thoughts when she looks this way. Better not to talk to her.

The stone, anyway, is the least of Fidanete's worries. If she were going to tug at her mother's hand it wouldn't be on account of that. Nor on account of her stomach, which rumbles now like an empty barrel; nor on account of Senat, her younger brother, who keeps poking her in the ribs with a stick he picked up near the creek whose path this road follows. None of those is worth troubling her too-troubled mother about, but her need for a bathroom might be.

Go in the bushes! There! Behind that tree! She can hear the impatience in her mother's tone, see the crease deepening across her mother's forehead. She can even hear her mother's thoughts. How did I get such a daughter? But Fidanete wouldn't beg for a bathroom if all she needed was to relieve herself. For that, she'd find a bush to hide behind. The problem is blood. She is starting to bleed now, her first period. And her mother doesn't know it.

How many times did she and Aferdita nervously joke about this? How many times did they tease each other? What would you do if it came at school? How about—in the market? Crouched in the alley behind Aferdita's house, they watched the older boys come and go from the café across the street. Him? No—he's too conceited. Him? Maybe. Together they giggled and gossiped, as the shadows of the buildings lengthened, and the women called the smaller children home. Now—who knows where Aferdita is. She is gone.

To Fidanete's right, the cough and grumble of passing trucks and vans; to her left, the roar of water over rocks. Behind and ahead, friends and strangers—walking, walking,

walking. Her jacket is short; it stops just shy of her hips. She untucks her shirt, letting its tail swing out below the jacket's hem, tugging at it roughly to pull it down as far as possible. Her mother frowns at her and shrugs. There are miles to go before the Macedonian border.

Be friendly.

After the video, your facilitator will open the floor to questions. A latecomer will appear. "Sorry. Sorry," she will say. Watch her laborious progress as she shakes out her umbrella and lumbers across the room, ignoring several empty places near the door in favour of a spot in the farthest corner, where she adjusts her bulk in the flimsy stacking chair.

"As volunteers, you must remember your role," the facilitator will insist. "I cannot stress this enough. You represent this organization. You cannot be seen to favour any party to the dispute, and you must not befriend any individual refugee. You must not take anyone home with you."

The latecomer will frown. "But I thought this was the point!"

"I am afraid you missed the earlier part of the presentation where we talked about the role of non-governmental aid agencies, but I'd be happy to…"

"No! I read about this." The woman's overstuffed handbag will clatter to the ground. "We are finding homes for refugees. We are coming friends with them."

Watch the facilitator's face as it closes like a shutter. "You are thinking of another program," she will say. "Not this one."

Notebook entry

Tutoring. Today, one kid came for help with a paper about the "great chain of being." Theory held that every creature, from the lowliest microbe to the most exalted angel, was linked in a vast hierarchy whose pinnacle and ultimate source was God. Some thinkers saw this as a static system; everyone had a place and should remain there. Others saw the chain as a ladder. It was possible to move up a notch, to better your position. My student thought the course was boring and the idea of the "great chain" was a great joke.

The paper was a mess. Disjointed, incoherent. I asked *Where's your transitional sentence?* I directed her to a composition text. "The writer develops ideas in chains, each thought carefully linked to what has come before it and joined with equal care to what comes afterwards." But the advice felt shallow and fraudulent. Is this really the pattern of thought—a simple line that gathers its strength link by link by link? Does anybody think that way?

Fidanete peels her sock off. A blister, plump as a pillow, swells on the ball of her foot. She pokes it. Her mother is unpacking, spreading out blankets. Rain shakes the sides of the tent, and the earth beneath them smells flinty and damp. Senat, already lying down, rolls onto his side in a fetal curl.

"Where is Burim?" His voice cracks. The "im" comes out as a squeak. Burim is their older cousin, a big, rough boy of nineteen—Senat's hero. He had a gun, which he said would keep them safe.

Fidanete has told her mother about the bleeding. Now, over her brother's head, they exchange glances. Her mother

tucks the covers up to Senat's chin, smoothing the hair off his
forehead.

"I don't know. Go to sleep."

Senat's thumb floats to his mouth, but then he remembers
his age and shoves it beneath his head.

"Come, Fidanete. You too. Lie down." For once, their
mother's voice is gentle. "Rest. Make sure you are warm
tonight."

The tent's thin walls provide no barrier against the noises
outside—people shouting, feet falling on damp ground, the
cheep of the reporters' cell phones, the static of shortwave
radios. Where is Aferdita, Fidanete wonders. Could she be
here, at this camp? Maybe she is huddling with her sisters in
her own tent. Impossible to say. Tomorrow, in the light, she
will look for her.

From her sock, she withdraws the stone. It is not much
more than a pebble, hardly more than a bit of gravel, with
nothing to distinguish it except the warmth it has stolen from
her own foot. She rolls it for a minute against her palm, then
puts it in her pocket.

Be enthusiastic.

After the presentation, allow yourself to be interviewed
to determine your suitability for various tasks. When
they ask you what you know about the Red Cross, do not
tell them *tainted blood*. When they ask why you are here,
tell them you want to help the refugees. Later, you'll be
invited to the military base where the refugees are
housed. There, you'll be given the regulation bib. Tie it
on. Ignore the person beside you who mutters, "We

ought to be wearing crescents. The cross does not have positive connotations to this population." March onward. Pretend to be a Red Cross Knight. Even if you feel like Don Quixote.

95

Notebook entry

At the base. They called me to do outdoor child care but so far, all the kids are inside. No—not all. There is a young girl, twelve or thirteen or so. She sits alone on the grass, knees drawn up to her chest, watching her brothers play soccer.

The pain these people must be feeling. So much has been lost. They do not know if they will ever return to their homes. And yet the children still skip and play soccer. The women still sit in groups and talk to one another. People still smile and walk about in the sun.

I'll bet they are bored. Day after day in this tiny compound. No books, no music. (Do they have radios or TV inside?) No work. Unless they are writers, I guess.

Among the things that Fidanete left behind in Kosovo: a stack of fashion magazines; a bracelet given to her by her favourite aunt; last year's jeans, getting tight; her old dolls.

Among the precious things she brought: Aferdita's phone number. She did not have to write it down. It does not take up room, except in her mind, where she says it over and over. To Aferdita, she is besëtar. Faithful.

Her fingers, in her pocket, circle the stone again and again. Smooth here, rough and jagged there—she has memorized its contours.

Her mother sorts through their clothing, stacking and re-stacking the meagre pile of shirts and undergarments as if to make them reproduce. Her frown has returned, deep as ever. They have not heard from Fidanete's father yet. He was supposed to join them.

96

"Is Aferdita's family in Canada? Will they come here, to this camp?"

"Who knows where they are? They could be anywhere."

They could be dead, she does not say. But Fidanete hears.

Be well-trained.

Accept the assignment for child care, even if you have never actually cared for young children. Arrive at the base, tie on your bib, and stride across the field with a box of crayons and paper. The children will flock to you like birds. One boy, already at age eight a vivid charmer and a flirt, will take a red marker and a sheet of perforated computer paper and produce a passable Canadian flag. He'll bend at the waist in a playful bow. "Welcome. Welcome to Canada." Watch as he grabs the arm of the boy beside him and sketches a convoluted snake that wriggles when its wearer flexes a bicep.

After the younger kids run off to play, the teenagers will come, their bodies hidden in their baggy clothes, their faces hidden by their bangs.

"What is address here?" one of them will ask. He wants to get mail from his friends. "You know the address?"

No one has bothered to impart this bit of information to you. Promise to get it before your next shift.

Notebook entry

Reading Forster. His distinction between flat and round characters.

How to tell a true story? If I write it as non-fiction, I get to include all the messy details. I don't have to package it in an artificial plot. I get to say what I see. But how do I prevent myself from flattening the characters, turning real people into caricatures, turning their lives into anecdotes? I don't want those kids to be anecdotes.

Write it as fiction then. Get at different, maybe deeper truths.

But who am I to write their stories? What gives me the right?

And fiction or non-fiction—they didn't ask for this. They don't get a choice. So am I not simply using them, either way?

Leave it to a volunteer to do that, R. would say.

Fidanete's father has arrived. His pants droop across his hips, and a scruffy beard darkens his jaw, but his eyes are the same shrewd green ones Fidanete remembers. He will fix every-thing. With her mother, he will talk, late into the night. With Senat, he will chase a soccer ball. With Fidanete herself, he will go to the Office of Identification and Relocation, to search for Aferdita.

The office is lodged in an old storage room and staffed by a translator and three pale-skinned young women with golden hair. Every morning, they roll back the sliding screen dividing the room from the corridor, and every evening, they shut it with a click, leaving the computers humming in the airless dark. These computers are the heart of the place. One stores the names of all the Kosovars in Canada, together with the cities they have gone to. Another links them to temporary camps in other countries—in Italy, England, Israel—across the world. Phones are available for calls, and all day long the hallway outside the office echoes with strategizing, arguing, laughing, weeping refugees.

"They can find anyone. Anyone," one old man insists. They found his nephew, in Holland, missing for two years.

"Hear that?" Fidanete's father says.

But things are not so simple. To begin with, he must secure permission to look for Aferdita in the first place. Standing to one side in the crowded hall, Fidanete listens as he negotiates through the translator with one of the golden ladies.

The golden lady's mouth is prim. "She is not a relative," the translator says. "We are not authorized to initiate searches for those who are not relatives."

Fidanete's father ignores him and smiles directly into the golden lady's face. "She is a relative," he insists. He beckons Fidanete, clamps his hands on her shoulders and pushes her toward the grille. Her cheeks burn. "Cousin to this one. Just her age."

The golden lady blinks. "All right," she says. "We will help."

Be respectful.

Dress, on the hottest day of the year, in a long-sleeved, Mandarin-collared shirt, a pair of black pants, and shoes with closed heels and closed toes, mindful of your facilitator's instructions that you must not offend anyone's modesty. Arrive at the schoolroom and say hello to the translator, who has been pulled from the ranks of the refugees. She will smile, shake your hand, wipe her own hand across a sticky brow, and wonder aloud if you have taken leave of your senses to dress as you have in this heat. She wears a sleeveless top and a miniskirt and as soon as the kids file in, she kicks her shoes off. Her toenails are painted scarlet.

Show up to your next shift in shorts.

Notebook entry

Why am I doing this, anyway? Maybe R. is right. Half the therapists I know are there because they want to address their own childhood trauma. Lots of the teachers I know are really there to get back at some high school teacher of their own. Most of the doctors I know spent a good portion of their first year in medical school diagnosing their own illnesses. *Physician, heal thyself.*

But surely it's more than that? Can't remember a time when the TV didn't beam war into the family room. Can't escape the knowledge of what's going on in the world, or the knowledge that sixty years ago Mark and I and some of our dearest friends might have been among the refugees, bundled with whatever we could carry, herded like cattle, branded like cattle— separated from our loved ones, separated from the place we called home. The chain of being is a loop as well as a ladder. There, but for an accident of place and time, go I.

Maybe we are there to serve our own needs. But among those needs is a need for connection. Is that such a bad thing?

The search does not go smoothly. Fidanete and her father have to wait their turn, and many others are ahead of them in line. One day, the computer crashes. Another day, the names and locations come up scrambled. On still another day, the machine spits out pages, but the printing is illegible, and the golden ladies take away the portable phones and close the sliding door.

Finally, they shoulder past the others at the top of the line and get inside the office. They enter Aferdita's name into the machine. The golden ladies talk softly to each other while they click and scroll, click and scroll. Fidanete stands a few feet back, her arms stiff at her sides and her heart pounding. Her father peers at the glowing screen and at the printouts, again and again, shaking his head, questioning the ladies, exhorting the translator, frowning. At last he turns away.

"She is not in Canada."

Fidanete reaches for the stone in her pocket. Not in Canada. Not in North America. Nowhere on this side of the earth. Is she anywhere imaginable?

"Where? In Pristina?"

Sighing, her father returns to the desk. This time there is gesticulating, shouting on both sides.

"We need more information," the translator says. "We cannot search without knowing more than this. We do not have unlimited resources. Country. Do you have a country? What was their destination?"

Her father's shoulders slump.

The golden lady's face is strained; she points to all the others, still in line. "Many people are waiting."

Fidanete's fingers close around the stone.

Her father turns, glaring at her. "Always this friend. Why
don't you care about what happened to your grandfather?"

She stares at the vinyl floor, dragging her foot. Her sandal
stutters.

"You don't see Senat brooding indoors. What is wrong
with you? Go! Play!"

Be selfless.

"This is not the kind of population we are used to
moving," your facilitator will say. "Ninety-eight per cent
of the adults smoke. Also many children. The Red Cross
is an organization devoted to health. So. Do we supply
them, or not? You see the problem. We gave them Nikes
when they got here. Everyone got new shoes. But the
boys don't want Nikes. They want Adidas. And the girls
want platform sandals."

Notebook entry

Tired. Fed up, too, with the smug do-gooders over there
at the base. Sometimes I think R. is right. Some of them
want to be congratulated for what they're doing. Some of
them congratulate themselves. You can almost see their
halos.

Feeling stuck with this piece. Story or essay or whatever it is. I write it one way, then write it the other. I resist
and resist. I split it at the root, then put it back together
again. Maybe it could work, but so far, it doesn't.

So tired. I'd love to fall asleep. Right here in this
chair. Thinking about S. Dead now, and I won't ever see
him again.

Grief. That's what it's about. Grief is what chains us together, chains us to this earth.

Working on a chain gang.

102 *The others are better at English. Even Senat is better than she is. He turns around and smirks at her whenever she makes a mistake. Fidanete's eyes drift to the window, covered over with a big map of Canada—partly to block the ferocious sun, and partly because they will use it later, during the geography lesson. Ever since they got here, they've been studying geography and talking about the weather. Do they talk about nothing else in this country?*

In two more weeks, her family will go to a place with a long name, where her uncle already lives. "Saint Cat. Saint Cathet. Saint Catheter," she stammers.

"Cath-er-nzzzz," the teacher says. "Saint Catherines."

In the evenings, after supper, Fidanete's father listens to the shortwave radio and spits his curses back at it. Her mother sits near the window, mending clothes. Outside, Senat kicks a soccer ball with the other boys, while Fidanete struggles with her homework. What is this place, Saint Catherines? Her mother tells her there are fruit trees there. Pears and peaches and plums. In the autumn, when they arrive, she will be able to eat apples from the orchards. Red and shiny, with crisp white flesh. A is for apple.

She reaches for the stone in her pocket. A is for Aferdita.

Be co-operative.

Arrive for your shift to find a big sign stuck to door of administrative office:

VOLUNTEERS: DO **NOT**, UNDER **ANY** CIRCUMSTANCES, OFFER GIFTS TO REFUGEES!

Beg for the backstory. It goes like this: One volunteer, overhearing some Kosovar women commiserating with each other about their appearance, bought one of them a box of dye so she could disguise the grey roots of her hair. Now every female refugee over the age of thirty-five is clamouring for L'Oreal or Nice 'N Easy.

Notebook entry

It's no accident we compare creators to gods. We take on ourselves a god's prerogatives.

But would the world be any better off, without us?

Charting "illuminating connections." That's the biographer's work, says Michael Holroyd. "Only connect!" said Forster.

The chain of being is tarnished, knotted, and broken. Would it be straighter, any truer, without our words— however inadequate a word is, to solder a world together?

On Presentations Day, everyone must identify and say something about a favourite animal, or food, or sport, or game, or place. Senat talks about soccer. Regulations, winning teams, predictions for the next World Cup. How did he learn these words? They roll as easily off his tongue as their father's Albanian curses. Fidanete presents last. All through the others' talks, her teeth chatter and her heart pushes hard against her chest. When she finally stands to speak, she has *to grip the desktop to keep herself from falling. But she does it. She finishes. All in English. No mistakes.*

Afterwards, the teachers clap, and congratulate them, and pass round presents wrapped in coloured tissue paper. Senat's is a softball. He shrieks and runs outside to throw it to one of the other boys. Laura gets a box of paints. Fatlume gets candy. Politely, she offers samples. Fidanete picks a yellow one and pops it into her mouth.

Her own package holds a set of hair clips—two shiny, gold-coloured barrettes.

One of the teachers brings a hand mirror so Fidanete can see herself. She turns her head and the clips catch the light. With her short brown curls swept back this way, she looks stylish, she thinks—like an American movie actress. Like a grown-up—not a child.

The teacher has a kind smile. "Pretty," she says.

An answering smile creeps across Fidanete's face, a complicated smile, like the taste of the lemon Lifesaver melting now under her tongue. Aferdita would have loved these barrettes. She would have wanted a pair herself.

Fidanete touches them lightly. "Flutur."

"In English?"

"But—ter. Butterflies."

She reaches in her pocket for the stone. Not much more than a pebble, hardly more than a bit of gravel, with nothing to distinguish it except the warmth it has stolen from her body. She rolls it against her palm.

Be understanding.

At the playground, empty your usual supplies onto the picnic table, watching the children swarm round. Notice a woman approaching with her daughter from across the field. When her child has settled into play, instead of wandering off, as the adults usually do, the woman will sit. She is close to your own age and, judging from her hesitant nod of greeting, shy. While you help the boys and girls to crayons and colouring books and teach them the English words for the objects the books depict, she will look on with an expression of longing.

One of the boys, whose English is already good, will banter with you, tossing a deck of cards into the air. The woman will grasp his arm and pull him aside. She will point to you and pluck at the neckline of her blouse. Meet her eye and she'll repeat the gesture. Look down. You are wearing an identification tag. All the volunteers wear them. Maybe she wants to know your name.

Tell her.

But she will shake her head. Her eyes will remain on you, wistful.

The tag is fastened around your neck with a gold-coloured chain—just a cheap link chain, the kind you see on bathtub plugs and key rings. A tawdry, worthless thing.

Worthless to you.

The woman will pluck at her blouse again and frown. Again, you'll shake your head, pretending not to understand. Lying. She will speak to the boy and he'll approach you and touch the chain, then point in her direction. She wants that chain, wants you to give it to her. "No," you will say, "No." Remembering that warning against giving gifts, conscious that you're supposed to wear your ID at all times on the base, embarrassed for her and for yourself, you'll bite your lip and turn away.

Notebook entry

106 *OED, fifth definition of the noun "volunteer." (Now obsolete.)*

a. A deliberate lie. b. A voluntary gift.

1678 Dryden. Kind Keeper III i. "Now will he lie three or four rapping voluntiers, rather than be thought ignorant in any thing." 1757 Mrs. Griffith. Lett. Henry & Frances (1767) I. 154. "I think myself vastly obliged to dear Harry for his obliging voluntier."

That woman on the base. The one who wanted my chain. I volunteered in Dryden's sense, not in Mrs. Griffith's. Wonder what R. would say about that.

Writing. Writing lives.

Gift, or lie?

Be humble.

Female Troubles

The Bay Centre for Birth Control is a small, squat building made of yellow brick. It sits back of the road behind
a stamp-sized yard, dwarfed and doomed by the gleaming
towers that surround it on all sides. An unforgiving sun
pricks my scalp as I tramp across the pathway to its
frosted glass door. My boyfriend leans against the low
stone wall near the street, whistling under his breath.

The waiting room is tiny, bare except for banners
advertising International Women's Day. A large chart
lists the names and failure rates of various contraceptive
devices. No safe sex posters here. This is the '70s, before
we knew about HIV and AIDS, when the worst consequences of sex were unwanted pregnancies, botched
abortions, broken hearts.

My feet itch in their canvas platform espadrilles, and
the waistband of my pale green polyester dress pinches
my skin. I chose this dress especially for the trip from the
suburbs to the city. After my appointment, Hal and I
plan to walk north, towards Bloor Street. We are going
out to dinner in Yorkville. Before boarding the com-
muter train, we studied the newspaper to find out about

the latest restaurants, and that same paper, the *Star*, was also my guide for information about this clinic. The article I read was reassuring. I know they will dispense pills to girls my age without their parents' permission.

A harried young doctor leads me to an examining room and asks how she can help. Her eyes sweep across the table with its shiny metal stirrups, then linger on the shelf behind it as she calculates whether or not she has everything she'll need for the obligatory pelvic exam. But today there will be no internal exam. As I bend to reach into my purse, marbles of sweat bounce down my spine. I pull a pink plastic packet out of a side compartment and show it to her.

"What's this? This is the pill, isn't it. It's not some kind of mini-pill. It will stop me from getting pregnant?"

"Of course." She hands it back, her expression bemused. "Where did you get it?"

I got it from Dr. Fernwood, my mother's gynecologist. I had been suffering from painful periods. My friends' doctors had given them codeine or extra-strength aspirin for the same complaint; I wanted something similar. While my mother sat smoking in the next room, I primly explained to Dr. Fernwood (an old friend and colleague of my father's, and a frequent guest at my parents' parties) that I did not want to go on the pill. I wasn't sexually active and I didn't want to take hormones. I'd been reading Ms. and *Our Bodies, Ourselves* and had a well-developed horror of the reputed side effects.

Dr. Fernwood ignored me. He lied. "This isn't the same as the pill," he said, his familiar voice smooth and buttery as an avocado. "Very low, very low, low dosage. And it will help you with those cramps of yours. Guaranteed."

I had to admit, it did help. Later, I overheard my mother say that she had put him up to it. She was scared I had started having sex. In our many conversations about this subject, she had always maintained that she'd support me, no matter what; in the end, though, the risk that I might become pregnant proved impossible to accept. To be fair, she probably just wanted to protect me, to prevent all my fine opportunities from vanishing down a diaper pail.

Eventually, of course, Hal and I did decide to have sex. But I had taken my mother's hidden message much to heart, and although I was curious, even eager, my passion for research was more powerful. I skimmed my father's medical journals, scanned them for ads. Dr. Fernwood's pill must have been a relatively new brand, because I had to plow through three or four glossy issues of the *New England Journal of Medicine* before I found its name. Still, at last, there it was—the soft-focus photograph of the pretty, carefree woman in flowing skirts, the swirling, blurry background of purple and gold, and in the fine print on the facing page, amidst an alarmingly long list of precautions and contraindications, the magic words I was searching for: *estradiol*, and *progesterone*, and most importantly: *oral contraceptive*.

Even then, I was not content. "I know what it is," I said. "But I'd still like to check, just to be certain."

"Sure," Hal agreed, good-natured as always.

That young doctor must have enjoyed a long, lusty laugh with her friends after her shift was over. But for now she calmly cuffed me, measured my blood pressure, listened for a minute to my heart. "Well," she said. "Seeing as it's already been prescribed, and you've come all this way, I might as well give you a few samples." She thrust the pastel packets into my hands like penny candy. "Just make sure you take it at the same time every day. No forgetting."

Vindicated, relieved, triumphant, I fairly skipped down the path as I left the clinic. There, on the buzzing street, under the indifferent glare of the glass office towers, Hal and I giggled and kissed.

"Probably it's all for nothing anyway," I joked, as we began our trek to Bloor Street. "Probably I'm not even capable of having kids."

"Oh, come off it," he said. "Of course you are."

That's how careful I was. That's how seriously I took the word *precautions*. How strong my need was to control my own life, every moment, every breath of it. How deep my faith, that such a thing was possible.

Barren 1. *of a woman: incapable of bearing children; infertile*.

For the past three years, my husband Mark and I have been trying to conceive a child. Coincidentally, during these same years, I've had problems with my periods. Heavy flow. Strange aches. My doctor is affiliated with the local teaching hospital, and for two consecutive visits I am seen by residents when I report for my annual Pap smear. "Do you think I might have fibroids or

endometriosis?" I ask the first one. "Oh, no." She shuffles through my file. "That's unlikely." The second reas-
sures me: "It's normal to get a change in your periods as
you age. Nothing's wrong."

This year, Mark is on sabbatical and I have taken a
leave from my job to write a novel. We are living in
another part of the country. An unusually early period
sends me to a doctor here. He listens to my story and
then somewhat reluctantly signs the order for a sonogram. "It might be a fibroid," he says. "But even if it is,
there's nothing we can do. Hysterectomy. That's it. And
if you're trying to get pregnant..." He shrugs. "It's not
really an option, is it."

No.

I prepare by drinking a litre of water. In radiology,
the technician slaps pale green gel onto my distended
abdomen. "You're too full," she says. "I'll let you go in
just a second." But she doesn't. The instant the white
plastic probe makes contact with my skin, something
strange leaps into view. Turning away from the frown
suddenly creasing her forehead, I force myself to
breathe. *What if...what if, by some miracle, I am pregnant?* But that's silly. I know I'm not. My period is due
in three days, and already my breasts are swollen and
tender, already I feel the usual tugs and stirrings, so
different, I imagine, from the tugs and stirrings of new
life.

The machine talks to itself in bleeps as the technician
probes my belly. I wince. Normally, I tolerate pain quite
well, am good at relaxing into it, but this hurts, it hurts

a *lot*, and I can't pretend. "I'll let you go in a second," she repeats. "Afterwards, come back. We'll need to take more pictures."

I peer into the monitor. There it is again, that strange swelling. She presses and it jumps closer, filling the screen. Two black spots cloud its centre, blurry around the edges like a pair of thick-lashed eyes. It looks like a baby seal.

"Have you ever taken follicle-stimulating drugs?"

I stammer, stupid with confusion. "Folic. Follicle? I've been taking folic acid. But that's not the same. Is it."

"No, that's not the same," she agrees, without looking at me.

When my parents were newly married, my father was still in medical school, and unable to support a child. Then, when he began his residency, they decided it was time to start a family. My mother tells me she had some trouble getting pregnant. In the language of the day, her uterus was "tipped." Supposedly, this made things more difficult. "We'd given up," she says. "I thought it wasn't going to happen."

"Then what?"

"Then…well…it did. But at first, I couldn't believe it. When I missed my period, I got scared. I thought there must be something wrong. It had to be something wrong. I thought you…I thought you were a tumor."

2. of an animal: not pregnant at the usual season.

The first time I had unprotected sex I was thirty-two years old. I was premenstrual that night, and so knew the odds of pregnancy were next to nil. In my twenties, I was ambivalent about having children, financially and emotionally unstable, unsure of my capacity to mother. At around thirty, I began to feel more confident that I could parent, but my first marriage floundered and then ended, and the relationship I entered afterwards was in its early years too improbable, too provisional to shelter a new life. And so I waited. In this I was not alone. None of my university-educated friends had children, either. All led similar lives; all asked themselves similar questions, interrogating their own fears and longings over and over again. We were the first generation to have taken the pill for granted, and the pill—whether we took it or not—drastically altered our experience, separating us from our mothers and even from our older cousins and sisters.

This year, my friends and acquaintances are having babies. A colleague my age, who miscarried last year, brings her next child to term and after a long and difficult labour, successfully delivers a son. Two of my best friends announce their pregnancies within weeks of each other. Another friend gives birth to her second daughter. My husband has adult children from his previous marriage; now he discovers himself a young grandfather. In this unusually early spring, a season of almost embarrassing abundance, I see pregnant women and babies everywhere—on the street, in the supermarket lineup, at the doctor's office, in my dreams.

"Technically, of course," my gynecologist says, "the best time to get pregnant is when you're sixteen or seventeen. It may not be the best time socially, but biologically…" His voice trails off. He is a few years younger than I am, not long out of medical school. Last week, he postponed our appointment because he had to stay home to care for his newborn twins. While we talk, he doodles on the pad in front of him. I can see the logo: a pharmaceutical firm based in my hometown. They manufacture birth control pills and spermicidal jelly. "We'll see what we can do," he finally says.

3. *of a tree or plant: not producing fruit or seed.*

I have a fibroid, Dr. Cooper tells me, a benign uterine tumor. Not uncommon, not ordinarily dangerous, but in my case, because of its size and location, a possible cause of infertility, since it appears to be irritating a portion of the uterine wall and may also be compressing the fallopian tubes. This fibroid, however, is the least of my worries. I also have a large ovarian cyst. It could be a normal, follicular cyst; then again, it could be an endometrioma, or perhaps a benign dermoid cyst; possibly it is cancerous. He will have to run more tests; I'll need another ultrasound.

If the cyst is not the normal, follicular type, the doctor says, I may not be releasing eggs at all. Or the eggs I do release may be unhealthy, incapable of implanting themselves in my already inflamed endometrial wall. On the other hand, they may implant themselves, but briefly, so that I miscarry at the very moment I would expect my period to arrive.

"It may be coming out in the wash," he explains. "So to speak."

4. of land: producing little vegetation; unproductive.

Since my first appointment with the gynecologist, I am finding it difficult to work. Every morning I go to my desk and switch on the computer; every evening I glance through my notebook and read the sketches and bits of scenes I've compiled for the novel I am writing. On the days when I manage to immerse myself in my imaginary world, work is a wonderful distraction. But most days, my characters remain as distant as they were before I dreamed them. Most days, I have trouble making myself care about mere words.

I surf the Internet instead. There are hundreds of "resources" for infertile couples. Doctors' home pages, links to Britain and Australia, books, chat lines and support groups, descriptions and fee schedules for expensive, controversial assisted-reproductive technologies. I find it overwhelming. One source tells me that at least a sixth of North American couples experience infertility, medically defined as the inability to conceive after a year of unprotected intercourse. Thirty-five per cent of the cases are "female factor" (the woman's fault, I can't help thinking), thirty-five per cent are "male factor" (how neat and equal, that division!). In twenty per cent of cases, both people have some difficulty, and the rest are "unexplained."

From what I understand, while each of us responds to this condition differently, each has her own way of adapting to it—or not. In general, our emotions are predictable. Shock, denial, guilt, rage, blame, bargaining, jealousy, depression—the usual catalogue of grief. "My life is meaningless without children," a woman says. "I am afraid my husband will divorce me," says another.

One fertility specialist in Atlanta almost seems to relish these expressions of despair for the contrast they provide to his eventual "happy endings." Dr. Perloe's laudable aim is to transform his patients from victims and "guinea piggies" into active participants in their treatment. Chapters in his online book include advice on "developing an individualized plan" and becoming "a positive force in your own fertility treatment." Yet despite the exhaustive and accurate information it contains, despite its upbeat slogans and its rhetoric of agency and control, his book is at bottom a fairy tale. The title, *Miracle Babies*, betrays its true genre. In it, Perloe plays the roles of wizard and prince, creating life where none was possible before, restoring the virtuous, who work and wait, to their illusion that they can do whatever they dream.

Well. Why not? He and other doctors like him *are* making people happy. Some of his patients get pregnant; some of the couples in his book are raising their children as I write. And however skeptical I feel, the stories tempt me. Reading them, I wonder: *What if?* Three years ago, the prospect of in vitro fertilization would have struck me as a self-indulgent mistake; now I weigh it as a possibility—and, for a fee of just over four thousand dollars, consider it worth every penny at the price.

Why do I want a child? Why does anyone? One infertile friend describes the almost "reptilian" ache she feels when she cradles someone's baby. "It's not jealousy," another friend insists. "Truly, it's not. But it makes me horribly sad."

I do not want a child to carry on the family name or the family business. I do not want a child to complete me or transform me into an adult. I do not need a child to look up to me now or look after me in old age. I want a child because finally, in my thirties, I have learned a few things about love and how to share it. I want a child because together, Mark and I would be good parents. That is all.

5. *destitute of interest or attraction; arid; dull.*

What must it have been like, one hundred, two hundred years ago or more, to carry the label *barren*? If they had the misfortune to marry a king, some of those women lost their heads. Some, taken for witches, burned. Some burned inside for shame, having failed to fulfill God's purpose. And others, with what sweet relief, must have tossed aside their stays, freed as no one else to be sexual, to lie with a man in hot embrace, unafraid of the childbed's fierce exhaustions and grave dangers.

These days, infertility ruins more sex lives than it enhances. I hear about people who blame their own bodies, who feel cheated and undone by their own flesh. I read about couples who pick fights as a way of avoiding "sex on demand," couples who fake the "X's" in their basal body temperature charts, lying to their doctors, lying to themselves.

This does not happen to Mark and me. Perhaps because, until now, we had no reason to suspect an ovulatory dysfunction, and so have not been keeping strict records, we look forward to the peak time of the month, make trying a kind of game. But when I first hear the word *hysterectomy*, as applied to me, something inside me falters. I picture my mother's friends. Some of them underwent the surgery twenty years ago, and I remember them then as impossibly old. In fact, they *were* older than I am now, but not by so many years. I begin to number each new gray hair, each tiny line. And then, after my first sonogram, the image of my "growths" feels inscribed into my brain, and when Mark leans over to touch me, I seem to feel their swelling more insistently.

I walk to the beach near our temporary home. The day is warm and clear, and the sand is crowded with sunbathers. Next to me lie two lovers, as entangled as the wild roses lining the path, her pretty brown calf slung across his hip, his dark head nestled into the crook of her silver-bangled arm. *Unfair, unfair*, I want to shout at them. I think of Roethke's line about a woman lovely in her bones, and wonder when, or if, that liquid sensuality will ever return to me—when, or if, I will ever again feel a glow, like pollen, beneath my skin.

6. *producing no result; fruitless; unprofitable.*

The blood test is negative. I don't have cancer. The second sonogram is a success. My cyst has disappeared.

Mark and I perch on a hospital cot to hear the news. Dr. Cooper sits below us in his sea-green surgical scrubs, a smile animating his freckled face. "I'll be honest with you," he says. "I didn't think it was going to turn out like this. I thought we were going to have to do surgery right away. That first ultrasound didn't look good."

In his relief, which is almost as pronounced as our own, he forgets for a minute that the "fertility issue" has yet to be resolved. Because, even as it demonstrates that my cyst was of the normal, follicular type, even as it reveals my perfectly ordinary ovaries, the second ultrasound also illuminates the fibroid. Still there, still growing, still a possible culprit in our failure to conceive.

"What are the options for treatment?" Mark wonders.

"Not great," the doctor admits.

There are drugs designed to shrink the tumor, but they are too powerful to take for any longer than six months, and their major side effect is unpleasant—an instant (if temporary) menopause—abrupt and for many women psychologically overwhelming, not least because it is counterintuitive. Menopause ordinarily marks the end of a woman's fertile years, so it is far from easy to accept this passage as fertility's potential beginning. Then, too, the drugs are expensive—about $450 a month, not covered by health insurance—quite a hefty price to pay for almost certain discomfort and an entirely uncertain result. Finally, apart from drug therapy, the only option is myomectomy, a surgical procedure to remove the fibroid. This carries all the risks of any major surgery, and as with the drugs, can at best be considered a temporary solution; whichever course of treatment is chosen, the fibroid will likely grow back within six months.

"You'd have a three- or four-month window of opportunity," Dr. Cooper says. "Three or four months to get pregnant. That's it. Then you'd be back where you started from."

The cost of infertility treatments can be enormous. Some people spend more than $30,000 in their efforts to conceive a child. They borrow from relatives or friends, take out second or third mortgages, factor the price of drugs into their monthly budgets along with food and rent and other necessities. And what of the social costs? The reluctance of public and private insurers to pay the bills for some procedures may be justified. An Indian source puts it most starkly: "There are already too many babies in this country. Why exacerbate the population problem by producing more?"

On the contrary, the authors of *How to Have a Baby: Overcoming Infertility* argue that each of us has a "biological right" to have a child, and the fact that our neighbours may have "too many" children is no reason to deny us our own. Moreover, infertility treatments are a "much more cost-effective use of resources than a number of other accepted surgical procedures," such as kidney transplants or joint replacements, they claim. No one objects to heart surgery for a seventy-year-old man whose life expectancy is only a few more years. Why cavil, then, over a few hundred or even a few thousand dollars spent to address the health needs of people in their thirties, who have their entire lives ahead of them?

Not everyone agrees with fertility doctors like these, of course. Many people feel free to pass judgement, telling us it's wrong to seek treatment. And those of us without children may be excused for a hint of bitterness about that. For, whether we choose our childless condition or not, we risk the appellation *selfish*. Meanwhile, assisted-reproductive technologies should make social and ethical theorists of us all. Reports of high-risk multiple births and of doctors or technicians inseminating patients with their own sperm, taking eggs and embryos without their patients' consent, or exploiting their patients with expensive, unsuitable, and often damaging treatments percolate in the media and in our collective imagination. Is this the kind of world we want to live in? Is this the kind of world anybody's children deserve?

7. of a person: unresponsive; dull.

Infertility is not a subject many people know how to talk about. The age difference between Mark and me and the existence of his grown children protect us from crudely jovial "About time you two started a family!" remarks. Yet even some of my closest friends turn insensitive when faced with this trouble they don't share. "Maybe it's for the best," one insists. "This way, you'll do more writing. Give birth to books." "But that isn't how you define yourself," another reminds me. "You have so many other roles. You don't really *need* to be a mother."

And it's true. I am lucky. In an unmarried aunt who worked, travelled the world, and never left off learning, I have always had a model of one way to live a childless life. I love and am loved by a good man, a man who knows how to talk, and who knows how to listen. I have watched his children blossom and thrive partly as a result of my care. My work as a teacher gives me further opportunities to counsel, encourage, and nurture. And I have solid, sustaining friendships with women, some of whom are writers who have chosen to remain childless—meaning I never need to fear that children will be all they want to talk about; meaning words, my first and most enduring love, will always find an echo.

Yet none of this erases my desire to bear and raise my

own child. No matter how I look at it, infertility is a loss, a painful, too-private bereavement. How am I to mourn something that never was? How grieve for what might have been—for what could have, would have, should have been?

For years, I owned an asthmatic cat. As he aged, his condition worsened, and one night I thought he was going to die. Lying beside him on the bed, listening for hours to the rattle in his lungs, then driving blindly to the vet's, sure that each weak gasp might be his last, I had a dim presentiment of the kind of pain a parent feels, forced to watch her own child suffer. Then, with treatment, the cat's health began by slow degrees to improve. Holding him purring in my arms, or watching him extend one delicate dark paw in a patch of sunlight on the carpet, I drew a breath of the pure, sweet joy that must rise inside a mother whenever she catches her own child unawares, and is permitted, for that instant, simply to see the child as she is—separate, unique, a whole and perfect self.

There is nothing duller than death, nothing more barren than a grave. We do not like to be reminded of infertility because, like any condition that cannot be cured, like any disease that can't be beaten, like death itself, it is permanent, and like death itself, it is out of our control. The Bay Centre for Birth Control was torn down many years ago, and in its place, one block west, the offices of the "miracle baby" doctors line the gleaming hospital towers. But we are all of us getting older, and all of us will die, and even our children and our carefully crafted books will outlast us only a little while.

At Lingyin Si

At Lingyin Si in the city of Hangzhou, women come to pray for fertility. Although the name, translated variously as "Palace of the Hidden Immortals," "Temple of Inner Seclusion," and "Temple of the Soul's Retreat," suggests an oasis of tranquility and calm, the place is wildly popular with Chinese and Westerners alike, and all day long its crimson halls echo with the snap, gaggle, and stomp of tourists. Zen monks remain in residence, but the clink of cash registers rings louder than the chime of prayer bells.

That does not deter the hopeful. On a hot September morning, I stood inside the temple gates with a friend and our newly adopted infant daughters. Together we watched as one young woman paid her respects to Guanyin, Goddess of Mercy. Dropping coins into a wrought iron urn, she gathered sticks of incense and laid them, smoking, at the altar. There they lay against a hill of fruit, flowers, and two- and ten-yuan notes deposited by other supplicants. The girl's sharp-edged haircut, fashionable clothes, and vivid makeup announced a modern sensibility, but the look on her face expressed reverence and fervent desire. Ignoring the pushing crowds, ignoring our prying eyes, she bowed and whispered her prayers.

Sensing a presence at my elbow, I turned. An elegantly dressed woman in her fifties, a stranger, leaned over the rim of the baby sling. "Girl," she said, gesturing to the sleeping child.

I nodded.

"You have to go through long process. In your country also."

"Yes."

"How much you pay the Chinese government?"

My friend and I exchanged glances. Adoptive parents do not relish the imputation of baby buying. I fussed with the carrier's straps, pulling my daughter closer and turning her face away from the stranger's. "A donation. To the orphanage," I said. "I put it in the director's hands."

"Ah. The *orphanage*." Noticing my coolness, the woman drew back. For a few minutes we spoke of other things—the heat, the pressing crowds. She asked my friend and me where we were from and told us that she came from Macao. She peered again at the two babies. "Pretty girls. Lucky girls," she remarked before continuing on her way. "Lucky parents," we corrected.

Several new tour groups entered the temple enclosure, their voices raised in animated talk, their colour-coded baseball caps bobbing. The young woman at the altar stood up as if to leave, but instead she went back to the iron urn, returning with another stick of incense.

"That was a strange question," said my friend.

I shrugged. "People have so many misconceptions."

At the age of one week, my daughter was delivered by local police to the Hangzhou Children's Welfare Institute. Located on the outskirts of the city, near the site of an ancient, unexcavated tomb, and surrounded by rice fields and orchards, the orphanage was largely rebuilt in 1994 after an earthquake damaged it badly in 1992. It stands on a 15,000-square-metre lot and includes eight large buildings and several smaller ones. With its pristine clinic, its brightly tiled turrets, and its playgrounds, fountains, and stone pandas nestled amid the poplars, the complex looks like a peculiar hybrid of hospital and fantasy theme park.

This is where my daughter spent her first ten months of life. I can only guess at the details; the Hangzhou Institute's "Brief History of Infants"—the record of our daughter's stay there—is less than a hundred words long. But from that document and my own short visit, I know a few things. I know that the cool light reflecting off the chrome cribs and the blue tile walls is the light she traced round the room. *Eye can follow the moving object to 180 degrees.* That here, from overworked young women dressed in white or pink lab coats, she learned what it is to be cradled in someone's arms. *Shy, quiet, like to cuddle* Here, she tasted formula and juice. *Feed every three hours, feed when needed, no fix time.* Here, she began the complicated tasks of motor and cognitive development. *When adult call her name, she can lift her head and look at the person.* Here, day after day, night after night, the coos and cries of other babies soothed and startled her.

Although they are not our children we take the responsibility of their parents, reads an orphanage brochure. To how many does the staff owe this responsibility? Before the earthquake, the institute held one hundred and fifty beds; more were added during the renovations. State orphanages like the Hangzhou Institute exist in every major city in China; altogether there are seventy-three of them, housing 20,000 children. In addition, smaller, privately run facilities and social-welfare homes, which shelter the infirm and old as well as needy children, are common throughout the country. Reliable statistics about the total number of orphans at any given moment are difficult to obtain, but estimates have ranged any-where between seventeen thousand and one million. A conservative figure, based on government sources, is 120,000.

Conditions at the orphanages vary. Larger institutions like the one at Hangzhou provide, at a minimum, clean clothing, clean bedding, a heated room in winter, and regular feedings of formula. But even a relatively well-funded orphanage like this one can be poorly staffed, and no matter how they try, two inexperienced and possibly untrained girls can't consistently meet the needs of thirty babies or more. In the worst orphanages, babies are strapped to potty seats for hours, fed formula stretched with dirty water, ignored for their "naughty" screaming, or worse yet, beaten or abused. And even in the best orphanages, they are propped in walkers or stuck in their cribs for most of the day. Before their first birth-days, these children have already undergone the acute stress of abandonment and the chronic stress of neglect. Most of them will never be adopted.

The Chinese have a saying: Above are the Halls of Heaven; on earth, Suzhou and Hangzhou.

Hangzhou's history spans more than two thousand years. Achieving prominence at the southern end of the Grand Canal during the Sui Dynasty between 581 and 618 AD, it was also the capital of the Wuyue State, and the seat of the southern Song Dynasty in the twelfth and thirteenth centuries. During this period, despite the bureaucratic factionalism of the Song court, China experienced unprecedented advances in agricultural technology and productivity, in commercialization and urbanization, in scholarship, literature, and all the arts. As the capital, Hangzhou was the hub of all this activity. Shortly after its prime, the Venetian merchant Marco Polo claimed to have visited the place, calling it:

the noble and magnificent Kin-sai, a name that signifies "The Celestial City," and which it merits from its pre-eminence to all others in the world, in point of grandeur and beauty, as well as from its abundant delights, which might lead an inhabitant to imagine himself in paradise.

A hundred miles around, the city was cross-hatched by hundreds of paved roads. Twelve thousand bridges spanned its numerous canals. Ten market squares and hundreds of shops sold every conceivable good: the textiles and ceramics for which China is justly famous, but also wood, pearls, and handicrafts from Japan, ginseng and other medicinal herbs from Korea, spices, ivory, and jewels from India and the Middle East, and even silver from Mexico and Peru. By the late thirteenth century, the wealthy population had swelled to nearly two million, and the city was renowned for its sybaritic life. Courtesans plied their trade in every quarter. Theatres, many of them with multiple balconies, played to packed houses in seventeen separate amusement districts. Residents spent vast sums on their houses, furnishing them with floors inlaid with precious metals, ceilings adorned with elaborate carving, and opulent brocade tapestries. People wore silk; pets were dyed pink with balsam leaves. And day and night, carriages traversed the avenues, while dozens of beautifully painted pleasure barges cruised the famed West Lake.

The management of arms is unknown to them, nor do they keep any in their houses. They conduct their mercantile and manufacturing concerns with perfect candour and honesty. They are friendly toward each other, and persons who in-habit the same street, both men and women, from the mere circumstance of neighbourhood, appear like one family.

At each stage of our adoption, Chinese officials bestowed a gift on our daughter. A silk scarf. A stuffed bear. A piece of jade. A chop, or traditional seal, engraved with her name. To my husband and me, they gave documents. Passport. Birth certificate. Adoption certificate. And another certificate, unnamed. Our institute has searched for her parents and relatives by all means, but no trace can be found.

No trace.

A partial fiction, spelled out to appease the Gods of Bureaucracy.

It is the custom of the people of Kin-sai, upon the birth of a
child, for the parents to make a note, immediately, of the day,
hour, and minute at which the delivery took place.

So said Marco Polo, almost seven hundred years ago.

Undressing my daughter for admission, orphanage workers discovered a piece of paper. On it, her birth date appears in simple, even crude-looking characters. Nothing more.

The existence of a note implies a literate parent, but the rough calligraphy suggests someone without much education—or without much time. Whatever her circumstances, this someone troubled herself to find or beg or borrow or buy a pen and a piece of paper. She folded the paper into a tiny square, buried that square within the folds of the squirming baby's clothing, searched for a place to set the child—and walked away.

Why China? some people asked us when they heard of our plans to adopt. Oh, *China,* said others. Of *course.* They throw their girls away there, don't they.

Lingyin Si was founded in 326 AD. At one time, it consisted of nine towers, eighteen pavilions, seventy-five halls—a total of three hundred rooms—and provided a home to three thousand monks. But in every century, war and other disasters have taken their toll; throughout its history, the temple has been destroyed and rebuilt at least sixteen times. Most recently, only the intervention of Zhou Enlai saved it from complete devastation at the hands of Mao's Red Guards.

130

As with Lingyin Si, so with the city where it stands. Europeans sneered at Marco Polo's account of Hangzhou as too fantastic to be believed—yet later travellers confirmed it. For many years, even after the invasion of the Mongol emperors who were Polo's employers, the city maintained its prominence. Gradually, though, its harbour silted over, and trade moved first to Ningpo and, later, to Shanghai. The fine canals and roadways fell into disuse and disrepair; the market stalls stood empty. Calamity struck in 1861, when Hangzhou was occupied by Taiping rebels, then recaptured by the Imperial army. In the ensuing fracas, the city was almost entirely destroyed and the bulk of its population was dispersed or killed.

The men as well as the women have fair complexions, and are handsome…

My daughter's complexion is fair and bright. Her cheeks flush pink with excitement, cool air, or anger. Her hair is fine and fast-growing, her features delicate and regular, her lips the kind that people sometimes call bee-stung. From someone, she inherited these gifts, and more—her responsiveness to music, her strength and superior balance, her talent for mimicry, her delight in words.

Inherited, too, is her temperament: not *shy, quiet,* as promised by the orphanage report, but active, expressive, spirited, intense. Content, she hums and babbles. Happy, she laughs, and her laugh strikes the air like a silver bell; there is nothing she likes better than to dance. Angry, she wails and thrashes. Only when frightened is she still.

131

Contemporary Hangzhou has regained much of its lustre. Arriving by air from Beijing, Mark and I saw first a green and luxuriant landscape. Then came houses, hundreds and hundreds of them, each more than four stories high, many of them bulging with balconies and capped with gleaming towers. Their tile roofs glistened in the sun like the scales of hundreds of fishes. Apartment buildings I assumed from their size, but the Chinese-born coordinator of our adoption agency assured me they were private family homes. "The tea," she said, gesturing back toward the rolling hills. "Farmers here are rich."

Indeed, Hangzhou is now the wealthiest city in Zhejiang, which in turn is one of China's wealthiest provinces. With a population of over six million in the greater metropolitan area, it is home to four new "state-development" zones, focusing not only on traditional strengths of the region such as textiles and food processing, but also on chemicals, tourism, and high-tech industry. In 2005, the contractual value of foreign investment in the area exceeded 5.38 billion American dollars, with more projected. These factors no doubt contribute to the astonishing rise in Hangzhou's gross domestic product and to the improved standard of living enjoyed by its inhabitants.

Hangzhou remains remarkable among urban centres in China for its green spaces and its human scale. The boardwalk surrounding West Lake and temples such as the Six Harmonies Pagoda and Lingyin Si do much to preserve the city's tranquil atmosphere. But this peacefulness is threatened by the pace of development. In Hangzhou's moist air, the sounds of ten centuries or more commingle—the slap of water against the hull of a barge, the whisper of tea leaves tossed in a bamboo basket, but also the clatter of mechanical looms, the crash of wrecking balls, the buzz of pneumatic drills. One morning, as Mark and I left our hotel, we noticed workers beginning to lay the first bricks in a long wall. By sundown, the wall, a block in length and over ten feet high, had been completed.

If you want to forsake a child, there are many places to do it. An alley, or a field, or a ditch will do. The end of a long road. In the midst of thick tea bushes.

My daughter was discovered at the entrance to People's Hospital Number 7. Hospitals are notoriously busy places. People come and go at every hour. Many are connected in one way or another with the government. As in most other countries, in China it is against the law to abandon a child; the penalties for being caught include fines of up to five thousand yuan—more than half the annual income of an average worker in Hangzhou—and forced sterilization. If you want to abandon your child, a hospital is a risky place to do it.

On the other hand, many of the comers and goers to a hospital are doctors and nurses—people whose job it is to ensure the preservation of health, people who have pledged their own lives to protecting the lives of others. A hospital *is* a risky place to leave a child. Risky for the mother. Not for the child.

To strangers also, who visit their city, they give proofs of cordiality…

City dwellers on the east coast of China are now used to the sight of foreigners, so in Hangzhou we did not encounter the surprised stares that would have met travellers from the West a decade or more ago. Instead, we were greeted with smiles and attempts to communicate. Somehow, between our pathetic few words of Mandarin and their schoolbook English, we managed. One afternoon, Mark wandered alone into a busy restaurant. Unable to read the menu, he tried as discreetly as possible to look at people's plates in the hope of finding something to his taste that he could point to. A young man sitting at a window table noticed him. "Would you like something to eat?" he asked, in English. He then described the offerings in some detail and invited Mark to share a plate of tea-smoked duck, one of the specialties of the house.

The sight of children evokes from the Chinese an even friendlier response. Evenings, on the West Lake boardwalk and on city streets, we watched as parents by the hundreds slowed their pace to match their toddlers'. Looking up, they met us with expectant smiles. *Isn't he wonderful*, their faces seemed to say. Clearly, they were used to seeing their delight mirrored in the eyes of others. After our adoption, we became the focus of the same kind of attention. "Chinese baby," people some-times said. With those who could not understand English, we often flashed a printed card explaining in Chinese that she was ours by adoption. And everywhere, in government offices, in parks, in restaurants, on busy streets, our daughter's face and our laminated card were passports to wide, enthusiastic grins, to renewed attempts at conversation, and to that universal sign of approval, the thumbs-up.

My daughter's birth mother kept her for one week. When she set the baby down, her body must have ached from the delivery. Yet already she knew the child was healthy and strong. *Cries loudly, has good appetite*, reads a notation on the orphanage documents. In seven days, she would have nursed the infant perhaps forty times, bathed her at least once or twice, tended to her raw umbilical stump, dressed her and swaddled her, rocked her to sleep, gazed for hours into her dark, as yet unfo-cused eyes.

If the baby cried when she walked away, her breasts wept milk.

Every father of a family, or housekeeper, is required to affix a writing to the door of his house, specifying the name of each individual of his family, whether male or female, as well as the number of his horses. When any person dies, or leaves the dwelling, the name is struck out, and upon the occasion of a birth, is added to the list. By these means, the great officers of the province and governors of the cities are at all times acquainted with the exact number of the inhabitants.

135

Paper, movable type, chopsticks, porcelain, medicine, the mariner's compass, the kite, the abacus, gunpowder, the multi-stage rocket. As any seventh-grader can tell you, the Chinese have invented many useful things. The Chinese may or may not have invented bureaucracy, but they embraced it early and practise it with zeal. In November of 2000, shortly after we returned to North America with our daughter, they conducted their fifth official census since the birth of the People's Republic in 1949. Five million pollsters set out by bicycle, car and foot and knocked on the doors of an estimated 350 million homes, asking a series of twenty-one detailed questions. How old are you? What is your ethnicity? Do you have a toilet? Does it flush? Demographers eagerly awaited the results of this survey. The 1990 census found a population of 1.13 billion; the official population today is 1.32 billion. But the accuracy of this count is in doubt. Despite a media campaign assuring citizens that their answers would not be used against them, census takers found it difficult to secure co-operation. Early in the process, even the *People's Daily* acknowledged errors. One of the biggest challenges confronting pollsters was obtaining a precise count of China's migrant workers—peasants who have fled the countryside's exhausted land in search of work in the smog-choked cities. At least one hundred million of them scuff the dirt roads in their cotton shoes. Possibly there are two hundred million, or even more. No one knows for sure. Their shoes leave soft prints in the dust—a slight wind can blow them away. Two hundred million. It is as if the entire population of the United States had disappeared without a trace.

At all seasons there is in the markets a great variety of herbs and fruits, and especially pears of an extraordinary size, weighing ten pounds each, that are white in the inside, like paste, and have a very fragrant smell.

Julie A. Mennella, writing in *Pediatric Basics*, argues that the base notes or flavour principles of a cuisine may be transmitted to a fetus through its mother's amniotic fluid, and then, later through her breast milk. Infants may therefore show an early and marked preference for the flavours most associated with their culture.

Zhejiang is rice country. My daughter loves rice, cooked any way at all, but especially in a congee made with pork and shredded cabbage, flavoured with ginger and garlic. Excepting rice, she rejects the bland. Bananas bore her. She turns her face away from the rubbery skim-milk mozzarella that a friend's baby adores. She prefers broccoli mashed with scallions, or a parsnip and carrot puree. She likes sour apricot, bitter cress, sweet apple, pungent onion, salty soy. At a street stall in Beijing, I discovered one of her favourites—yam, roasted over coals until its skin turns black and its centre softens to a sticky pulp.

Yam. Hardy enough to thrive in times of famine. China's poorest food.

Mao encouraged the people to procreate. A peasant himself, he believed that a strong China would need to be a big China. The results were disastrous. As early as 1956, Zhou Enlai was urging limitations on childbirth, but until the late '70s less sensible voices prevailed, and throughout the '60s and early '70s many families had as many as five or six children. Meanwhile, rapid and badly planned industrialization was shrinking the arable land mass, already half that of the United States. By the time the Chinese government decided to get serious about population control, the situation was dire. Many officials and economists of that period would have been adolescents or young adults during the famines of 1958 to 1961. Then, an estimated 30 million people died of starvation brought on by crop failure due to the misguided agricultural reforms of the "Great Leap Forward." Half the casualties were children under ten. If you look at a population graph from the 1990 census categorized by age and sex, you will see that young adults aged 28 to 32 form the waist of an hourglass. That is the cohort who were babies during the famine years. Against this background, the one-child policy came into being.

Beginning in 1979, couples were limited to one child. Women who became pregnant without permission were subject to forced abortion, even in the third trimester. Over-quota births were punished with heavy fines and sterilization. Over-quota children could not be registered for schools and did not qualify for other state services.

And parents who flouted the rule lost valuable housing and medical subsidies.

Yet the one-child rule was never *just* a one-child rule. From the beginning, members of minority groups were permitted two children. And later, while urban and suburban Chinese remained limited to one, the rule was relaxed for rural dwellers. For them, "two children, one son" became the norm. Moreover, the policy was not equally enforced. In some areas, women's menstrual cycles were posted in the workplace, and if they did become pregnant, they might be dragged from their houses in the dark of night and injected with drugs to kill the fetus. In other places, cadres looked the other way when they learned of additional pregnancies, or imposed only minor penalties. Eventually, as economic conditions improved, wealthier families simply paid the fines and had as many children as they wanted.

Has the one-child policy worked? Opinions are mixed. Urban and educated Chinese generally support the rule as necessary for continued economic prosperity. But some Western analysts argue that the population would have stabilized on its own, and that nothing can justify the human rights abuses that the policy has given rise to. For now, the government has put the policy under review and is biding its time, promoting family planning.

Mark and I met our daughter in a hot, humid government hall. It looked more like a primary-school gym being readied for a Christmas dance. Rows of red plastic

chairs and gray Formica tables, bolted to the floor, faced
a raised proscenium. Red and green lights dangled from
the ceiling. Whirring fans failed to cool the air or muffle
the cries of thirteen other babies. Most parents in our
adoption group had met their children on the previous
day in a private reception area of our hotel; bureaucratic
inflexibility had prevented that for three other families
and for us. We were here now to sign official documents
as well as to see our daughter for the first time. All we
knew about her was written in that short "History of
Infants" provided by the Hangzhou Children's Welfare
Institute. Could we trust the information there? Within
minutes of our first glimpse of her, we would be required
to dip our thumbs in red ink and formally accept her as
our own. No turning back.

We waited. And waited. And waited. She'll be here
at nine, we were told. Then ten. Ten-thirty came and
went. The minutes passed slowly. We drank the bottled
water supplied by government officials. We crossed the
road to our hotel to retrieve forgotten articles. We
watched the other families with their babies and
snapped photographs.

"There she is," Mark said at last.

"That's not her." She was the only baby left, the final
arrival, and still I failed to recognize her. Could the
fragile, alert-looking fairy of our referral photo have
turned into this large and slack-faced child? I sought her
eyes; they seemed expressionless. Suddenly someone
thrust her into my arms. My muscles tightened beneath
the unaccustomed weight. "Mama," people were saying.

"Mama." We stared at each other. She did not struggle. She did not cry. Instead, she turned her gaze to my lapel and began to finger the brooch I had attached there, a small Canadian flag. Then, in terror no doubt equal to my own, she slept.

In their domestic manners they are free from jealousy or suspicion of their wives, to whom great respect is shown...

Respect is a relative term. Conditions for women were hardly advanced in Marco Polo's Venice. And throughout history, women in China have fared even worse than they fared in other countries. For centuries, Chinese men, from the loftiest philosopher to the humblest servant, were united in their sense of superiority over the opposite sex. Confucian society was patrilineal—control of the land and all property passed from father to son. In return, a son worked the land or continued in the family business, ensured that the ancestral spirits were properly worshipped, and cared for the parents in their old age. In many families, a daughter was perceived as nothing more than an extra mouth to feed. "Girls are maggots in the rice," goes an old folk saying. When daughters married, their names were struck off their own family ledgers and entered into their husbands'. From cradle to grave, women were expected to obey: in childhood, their fathers; in youth and middle age, their husbands; in widowhood, their sons. A woman's highest purpose was to produce a male heir. And despite changes in the political system and a slow improvement in attitudes toward women, in a land where social security remains a dream for most, sons are still required.

Names matter. They matter especially to parents, for by naming, we express our dreams and our desires, and declare a child our own. But adoptive parents of Chinese children ask themselves not only, *What shall we call her*, but also, *What has she been called—and by whom?* We wait by the phone with pen and paper and ask for a translation, or with characters in hand, we call up a Chinese-English dictionary on our computers and try to make sense of what we see. *Zhen Juan (Precious and Beautiful)*. *Qing Yuan (Clear Spring)*. *Xia He (Summer Lotus)*. Chinese names are often rich in poetic association, but for English speakers they can be difficult to pronounce. Also, in most cases, orphanage officials rather than birth parents have bestowed them. Even so, adoptive parents commonly retain these names. Whether or not they are actually used, they represent an important link to the past. Sometimes, though, to preserve that link in a way that we can accept, parents are forced to choose a Chinese name different from the one originally assigned. The translation of one adopted daughter's name turned out to be *Should Have Been Born a Boy*.

If my daughter's birth-mother named her, she kept that name a secret. *Jin Liang* is the name the orphanage director chose. Jin, meaning *gold*, and liang, meaning *virtuous* or *good*, together connoting someone who is excellent or outstanding. Good as gold. *Maia* is the name we added. From the Sanskrit: *creative power*. From the

141

Aramaic: *water*. From the Roman: *springtime, growing*. From the Greek: *mother*.

All over the world, all through history, hard times have led to infanticide. But few places on earth have known hard times like China's, or documented those hard times as China has. And when babies have been killed in China, overwhelmingly, they have been girls. During the early years of the one-child policy, female infanticide, having been almost unknown for years, began again in earnest. The practice was harshly condemned by the state but, as historian Jonathan Spence notes, "the very harshness of the critique hinted at the scale of the problem, believed by some Western analysts...to be in the region of 200,000 female babies a year."

How do they die? They are plunged headfirst into ice water at birth, left on hilltops in hot weather, or smothered in bedding, their cries silenced. In one Anhui village alone, forty girls were drowned between 1980 and 1981. For families with money and education, a more palatable option is available. The new technologies of ultrasound and amniocentesis allow couples to identify the sex of a child before birth. International Planned Parenthood estimates that despite laws that forbid sex screening, 500,000 to 750,000 unborn baby girls are aborted every year.

The result is a serious population imbalance. A natural population ratio is about one hundred and five boys to every hundred girls; in China today, there are approximately one hundred and twenty boys for every hundred girls. Already, the effects of this are being felt. Stories about the abduction and sale of women circulate in the hutongs and on the news; even the government has acknowledged the problem. On the boardwalk in Hangzhou, I saw scores of toddlers clinging to their parents' shirttails. I can count the girls I saw on the fingers of my hands.

Pregnant friends have reported that they often dream of babies. I dreamed of my daughter only once, eighteen days before she was born. I wrote the dream in a journal and then forgot its details. In preparing to write this essay, I read the entry over—then caught my breath, and read it again, and again.

The baby in my dream lived in an institution where the floors were made of linoleum and the light was aquarium cool. She was larger than I expected, sad-faced and silent, her body limp and heavy with grief. She could pull up and stand, but she was not yet walking. When I met her, she wore a blue-and-white jacket that buttoned up the front, blue pants, and slip-on shoes.

On the day the orphanage director handed her to me, my daughter met this description exactly. And, exactly like the baby in my dream, at the sight of our reflections in a mirror she met my eye and smiled. Later, when I held her to a window, she laughed as if she understood the language of the rustling leaves, then turned to me to share her rising joy.

According to a Chinese folk tale, an invisible red thread connects lovers who are destined to meet. The thread may tangle or stretch, but it can never be broken. Adoptive families have appropriated this story to explain the uncanny bond we often feel with our new children—the way, from the moment we meet, and sometimes even before that, we recognize them as our own. After a week in our daughter's company, Mark joked, "She likes to eat, and she likes to talk. She's come to the right family." He said, "Square hands. Strong legs. Just like her mother." And it's true. From the beginning, our similarities stood out. She sits with one foot tucked under her, snuggles against soft fabrics, minds the heat more than the cold, loves books, talks to herself, sighs with pleasure when a south wind tickles her cheeks.

Can we ever accurately read the expression in a baby's eyes? On our first night together, just before she fell asleep in my arms, Maia gazed at me for a long and solemn moment. She'd been fretting—tugging at her eyelid and scratching her ear, pulling on her hair, waving her fingers in front of her face, even grinding her teeth. Who or what was she missing from her former life? I had no way of knowing. Suddenly, she stopped fussing and fell completely still. Her eyes on me, intent and unblinking, appeared to be taking my measure. *This is it*, they seemed to say. *You're the one. Let's begin.*

This is it, my own eyes answered. *You're mine. I'm yours. Forever.*

The stranger leaning over the baby carrier's rim at Guanyin's shrine was not the only person who questioned my friend and me about our adoptions on the day

we visited Lingyin Si. Later, as we wended our way
through the shaded stone paths towards the exit, a crowd
drew round. Amid the coos and sighs of the women, a
young man's voice rang out, clear and emphatic: "Why
do you adopt a Chinese baby?"

How to answer that question? Should I tell him about
my desire to parent a child, my years of infertility, the
decade or more I might wait to adopt an infant in my
own country, my long-standing interest in Chinese
culture? Here, in this ancient garden, surrounded by
hundreds of Chinese, in the midst of a thriving city I
might never have known the name of had I not adopted
this child, my "interest" was exposed as pitifully unde-
veloped—a paltry thing.

I could not read his tone. Was he suspicious, even
hostile? I had heard that some Chinese mistrust the
motives of foreigners who adopt, fear that these children will be mistreated in their new homes. Did that
kind of doubt lie behind his question? Since my arrival
in China, no one had come closer to challenging me.
And if it was a challenge, it was not the first such challenge I had faced. The ethics of international adoption
are ambiguous at best. Some people argue that it is
never in the best interests of a child to remove her from
the country and culture in which she was born. They
argue that the practice of international adoption dis-
courages sending countries from doing more to find
solutions to the social problems that give rise to the
pool of adoptable children within their borders. They
argue that whatever safeguards and regulations are put

in place, international adoption amounts to nothing more than relatively rich people taking children away from relatively poor people. And then there are those—legion in our society—who, deep in their hearts, see adoption as an inferior way to form a family. I hear their voices in supermarkets, at the playground, even in my living room. "Such a *kind* thing you are doing," they say. And, "What do you know about her *real* mother?"

Whatever the rights or wrongs of international adoption, even its critics would acknowledge that it is far from the most exploitative practice perpetrated by the rich West against the less developed countries of our world. In December, 2000, the *Washington Post* published a story about blood harvesting in China's Anhui province. Anhui is poor and isolated, so its gene pool is unusually stable, making it a rich source of scientific data. But traditional Chinese beliefs militate against the donation of blood or organs, so even the poorest peasant requires incentives to give them away. In this particular project, Harvard professors and Chinese government officials promised desperately needed health care in exchange for blood, health care that participants claim was never delivered. Instead, unbeknownst to them, their DNA was being collected to help multinational drug companies in the West develop new products. The blood is banked in university and company labs, a resource for future study; meanwhile, the peasants themselves are no healthier, no wealthier, no better off at all. Yet, if this story is true, their loss may turn out to be a gain for yet another population, one entirely overlooked by researchers and participants alike. The "invisible red thread" that adoptive parents talk about may be visible, after all. Someday, for the thousands of children adopted in Anhui province, it may lead back to their "real" mothers.

"Why do you adopt a Chinese baby?" The young man's expression was dignified and serious. His was not an idle question. He deserved an honest answer. But what to say? I looked at my daughter, still sleeping. Her head was tipped back. Her cheeks were softer than a peony blossom. Beneath their closed lids, her eyes briefly fluttered and then fell still. "Because we love her," I said at last. He smiled broadly then, and gave me the thumbs-up.

Lingyin Si stands facing a beautiful hill, called Feilai Feng, "The Peak that Flew from Afar." The mountain is famous for its limestone carvings—in particular, one of a laughing Buddha. Many, of course, are restorations, but tourists in search of original work can climb the steep stairs cut into the rock face and search amid the nooks and crannies. When we visited, our tour guide recommended one such walk. Wearing the baby in the sling, and oppressed by the heat, I felt unable to make the climb, so I stood below while Mark went on with the camera. Workers were harvesting ginkgo, and the rattle of nuts and their peculiar stink permeated the air. Our daughter woke, and I bent my face toward her, babbling in the silly language of mothers and babies everywhere, oblivious to my surroundings. The world shrank to a small point—the tip of her nose, expanded to an ocean's depth; the orbs of her eyes. I looked up at last to find us surrounded. Half a dozen young women crowded around, giggling and flipping their hair. When they saw that I had noticed them, they squeezed closer. Their boyfriends stood apart, taking pictures of them with the baby and me.

"Do you think they pray only for boys?" my friend had asked me earlier, as we watched the young woman bowing to Guanyin. And yet, that morning on Feilai Feng, Maia wore pink.

Abandoning parents are understandably reluctant to talk about what they have done, so little is known for sure about their circumstances or their motives. But research suggests that the typical abandoning parents are average in almost every respect: a married couple in their mid-twenties to late thirties, with an average income for their area and an average level of education. Fifty per cent of the time, the husband makes the decision to abandon, while forty per cent of cases are decided by both parents. Birth-mothers alone, in-laws, or other family members decide the remaining cases. The typical abandoned child is a healthy newborn girl with one or more older sisters and no brothers. In their eagerness for a son, many families do abandon female infants, but most do so only after they've already reached or exceeded the quotas.

The week she turned one, Maia spoke her first English words: "boot" and "up." I like to think that the coupling foretells something about her character: feet firmly on the ground, but arms stretched to the sky, the better to catch her dreams. In the two months following her first birthday, she learned to climb up and down stairs, to clap her hands, to eat with a spoon, to bend over and pick up an object, to run, to "feed" a doll, to spin around until she fell dizzy and laughing to the floor. By then, she spoke dozens of words—so many that I had almost given up counting. Her birth mother witnessed none of these milestones.

Lingyin Si, the Temple of the Soul's Retreat, is only one of Hangzhou's many attractions. The city is also renowned for its fine silks, its Longjing tea, its beautiful lake—and its beautiful women. One million of them walk the causeways and ride the barges in the evenings with their husbands and boyfriends. They stamp documents, ring up sales, teach classes, diagnose illnesses, wait on tables, harvest rice. And they vacuum the floors, straighten the sheets, and assemble the portable cribs in the five-star hotels where Western adoptive families stay.

One million. Three million in the greater metropolitan area. Those are the ones the census managed to catch.

It is the custom...with the indigent class of the people, who are unable to support their families, to sell their children to the rich, in order that they may be fed and brought up in a better manner than their own poverty would admit.

No trace.

The soul retreats in the face of mystery like this.

Push-Me-Pull-You

A holiday weekend, and I am walking with my daughter to the park. She is not quite five. She sniffs the air like a young filly and canters into a pile of leaves.. "Hello!" she whinnies to every stranger we pass. "Happy Thanksgiving!" And even, "You look beautiful today!"

I set my face in what I hope is some semblance of a smile. This smile is my shield for what I know will come next: "How adorable!" "What a sweetheart!" "How old is she?" And of course, the inevitable "You are so lucky!"

When we reach the park, Maia wants me to push her on the swings. Her hair streams out behind, a black banner glinting with red highlights. "Now you get on, and I'll push you," she commands. She is strong enough to do it, too, though she forgets to get out of the swing's path on its return, and I have to stick my legs out and drag my boots in the sand so I don't slam into her. She laughs. "You stay sitting and I'll come join you," she says. She clambers up and positions herself face to face, astride my lap. Snuggling closer, she rests her head against my shoulder. "Swing, please. Rock me." This is an old ritual of ours, one begun when she was still a baby.

I croon her favourite lullaby. When she looks up into my eyes, her own eyes shine with the purest trust and affection. "You're the best mum in the whole universe," she whispers. "I love you to infinity and beyond."

I am so lucky.

That night, after I've read stories to her, brushed her teeth, cuddled under the blankets and banished the monsters from the closet, I tuck her into bed and lean across for a goodnight kiss. But instead of the soft pressure of her lips or the butterfly's brush of her eyelashes, I feel her small hands come up around my neck. Her thumbs are at my windpipe. She squeezes. Hard. I wonder if I am imagining this, if she's really just trying to hug me in some new and original fashion. She's creative and dramatic and physical and she likes to invent all kinds of games. Surely she's just fooling around. She doesn't really know what she is doing.

But she does know; she knows *exactly* what she is doing. She wants to choke me. To choke me.

Maia is the human embodiment of Dr. Doolittle's Push-Me-Pull-You. Dr. Doolittle is what I privately name each of the so-called experts whom I consult in search of explanations and help. These are the labels they try on and cast aside, for none of them fits exactly or covers completely:

Difficult temperament
Regulatory disorder
Sensory processing disorder

Attention deficit hyperactivity disorder
Non-verbal learning disability
Gifted, with asynchronous development
Unresolved grief or loss
Oppositional defiant disorder
Post-traumatic stress disorder
Reactive attachment disorder

Many, if not most, of her more challenging behaviours can probably be traced in one way or another to her early abandonment. In public, she plays two roles. At times, she's the poorly governed wild child. At others, she's the beautiful, exuberant charmer, perhaps a shade too friendly with strangers, perhaps a bit too "busy"—but precocious and delightful, just the same. Meanwhile, at home, we see the complicated self beneath the masks.

Living with Maia is like living in a hurricane zone. You can't relax because you're always scanning the sky for signs of trouble. Winds are generally high, and it's hard work at the best of times to clean up the falling debris. And when the storm breaks, it's all you can do to keep yourself intact in the face of its fury. Unless, of course, you find yourself within its calm, still centre. The hurricane's eye surprises even the weariest with hope.

Her first year with us was relatively easy. She was active, yes—unusually so—but just as the orphanage's paperwork had noted, she liked to cuddle, loved to laugh, and made good eye contact. Encouraging signs, and we felt encouraged by them. Even during her second year, warnings of trouble were subtle, mutable, and easily missed. All two-year-olds throw tantrums. Most four-year-olds don't, though, or not often. And if they do, their fury stops somewhere short of compelling them to fling chairs across the room.

She spins, hangs upside down, jumps down hard onto harder surfaces, and shows other evidence of early deprivation to her proprioceptive and vestibular systems— those subtle but all-important senses that tell us where our bodies are in space and help us to maintain our balance. She suffers from subtle developmental delays she did not establish hand dominance until she was nearly five. She struggles to sit still; she chatters and asks countless nonsense questions. Driven by impulse, she grabs and interrupts. She resists or defies almost every parental instruction, and can be so peremptory with us that we have nicknamed her "Miss Bossypants." Yet at the same time she demands our constant attention. Until she reached the age of four, she could not bear to be in a separate room from me if we were in the same house. Our recent move across the country has thrown her back to that emotional territory, and if I happen to leave her side now without repeated warnings, she screams.

And often, in the guise of seeking closeness, she aims to harm. "I'm sorry," she will say, after landing an elbow in my stomach, after leaping headlong and unannounced into my arms, after cutting me off and tripping me up on the sidewalk. "Ouch," I shout, as she plonks herself into my lap and the top of her head hits my jaw. "Oops," she says. I can't tell if that's a smirk on her face or a smile. She doesn't, yet does, want to hurt me.

153

And why shouldn't she? The person she was closest to in all the world deserted her shortly after she was born. The fact that her birth mother may have made that decision under enormous social or economic pressure, at great personal cost, and with only her baby's interests at heart is irrelevant to Maia. Deep in her cells, she knows only this—at the age of one week, she was left, helpless and alone. Then she was institutionalized, where, despite the best intentions of the harried staff, she was neglected and unloved for ten long months. Finally, she was handed off to a pair of weird-looking, strange-smelling strangers and taken a whole world away from everything known and familiar. And all this without explanation and entirely without choice. She was powerless, and being powerless felt bad, and now that she has finally gained some small measure of security and safety in our family, she never wants to feel powerless again. Hence her constant jockeying for control. She hones her considerable charm, sharpens her wits, and strengthens her will for violence. Far below consciousness, in the primitive part of her brain, she knows her survival is at stake. And her anger—the anger that should rightfully be aimed at her birth mother or her birth-father or the nannies at the orphanage; at a sexist culture or oppressive family-planning laws or long-standing customs militating against domestic adoption in China; or, perhaps most of all, at the vast global network that permits middle-class Westerners like me to whisk children like her away from their countries of origin—all that anger, the full fierce force of it, she points directly at me. At the person who, however guilty of participating in an ethically questionable system, is also the one who feeds her, bathes her, diapers her, teaches her how to walk, teaches her how to read, sings to her, plays with her, holds her, comforts her.

And loves her. Loves her. Loves her.

I live with a level of uncertainty about my mothering that is unusual even among the other adoptive parents I know. I am never entirely sure where I stand.

Around age two and a half, Maia went through a phase of aggression towards other children. Or, more precisely, towards babies. At her preschool, at our kinder-gym, at the park, even in our own house—whenever she saw a crawling infant, she would stomp over to him, loom above him menacingly, and then, with a glazed, cold, almost inhuman expression on her face, shove him to the ground. Snatching up the latest victim and rocking him, his mother might scold, "You need to set firmer limits. Give her some consequences!"

"There, there," others would sigh. "It's all because you are too strict with her. She needs you to be more nurturing."

"Never mind," counselled a third group. "All kids do that."

Or, in its nastier form, "What are you worrying about? She's normal. You're the one with a problem!"

Any way you look at it, I'm to blame.

I've seen those baby books in which proud parents are supposed to record developmental milestones. First tooth, first step, first word.

The milestones I should have recorded, but didn't:

> First kiss not flinched from
> First time she played for more than two minutes
>   on her own
> First adult conversation she allowed to proceed
>   uninterrupted
> First time she did not shriek in fury when I left the
>   room
> First time she could play quietly on her own beside
>   me
> First time she co-operated immediately with a
>   parental request
> First time she did not explode when a parent
>   refused a demand
> First time she truly relaxed

Then again, maybe it's better we didn't record these. The first step and the first word are assumed to lead naturally to the next and the next and the next. A simple, reassuring linear progression. But just because Maia did not explode when I disciplined her last week is no reason to think that she won't explode today. Just because she has accepted a kiss in the past is no reason to believe she won't brush it off tonight.

At the age of four, Maia told me, "I had a nightmare about a mean mummy with mustard teeth. And she was always mean to me. And I sang a happy song and put her in jail and then my nice mummy came back. But the mean mummy looked just like you except she had mustard teeth."

With Maia, normal parenting does not work, or does not work reliably. Although Maia understands the relation-ship between cause and effect, between her actions and their repercussions, she often cannot stop herself from doing what she knows she should not. Mark and I must become a species of super-parent, the "therapeutic" parent. We're not just here to raise her, we're here to *heal* her. The Drs. Doolittle agree that what children like Maia need is "high structure / high nurture" parenting; sadly, they agree less on the precise meaning of that term. Consistent consequences, or paradoxical reac-tions? Time-in or time-out? *Love and Logic* or *1, 2, 3 Magic?* Boot camp with bottle-feeding, is what it some-times feels like. What it doesn't feel is natural. The learning curve is steep and I don't have my climbing equipment.

I know we are not perfect. No parent is. But I know our parenting is at least as good as that of the smug know-nothings who sneer as I drag Maia kicking and screaming out of the park. Because I am Caucasian and Maia is Chinese, people don't always recognise immedi-ately that I'm her mother. In the face of what the good doctors would call her "negative persistence" and the seeming absence of a parent, people sometimes feel free to treat her rudely. "Stop that," they say, in tones I know they would never use with their own children. In tones they would never *need* to use with their own children.

When they learn that I'm her mother, they can barely contain their contempt. I want to scream at them. "Do you think you could do better? Go ahead. Give it a try. Be my guest."

I find myself a therapist. Nobody knows what to do for Maia, but maybe somebody can help me. The therapist asks me to find some pictures of "mothering." For a full week, despite the fact that I look and look and look, I do not see images of mothering anywhere. Or none that strikes a chord.

How can this be? My entire existence is focused on the task of parenting this child. The only other area of my life to which I have ever brought this degree of intensity and determination and pure passion is my writing. And now writing is a dim second. As for my marriage—well, the less said, the better. I never expected it to be this way. Mark and I were happy. We were friends as well as lovers. Together, we'd weathered thirteen years of highs and lows, thirteen years of boring work and fulfilling work, thirteen years of sicknesses and the return of health, thirteen years of trips, and money problems, and family problems, thirteen years that even included co-parenting his older children through their teenage agonies and angst. And still we had energy to spare, enough to want to raise a child from babyhood together. Now, when we're not fighting about how to handle our daughter, we lie conked out, exhausted, in the wake of her demands. I recall once hearing a friend say that her sons occupied a far bigger place in her life than her husband. At the time, I felt appalled and faintly self-satisfied. That will never happen to me, I thought. And maybe it wouldn't have, if our daughter had been different.

One summer day when she was five, Maia and I accompanied a friend and her daughter, Emmie, to our local wading pool. While my friend and I sat talking under a shade tree, the girls splashed happily in the water, taking turns giving one another rides on a plastic float toy we'd brought along. Soon another girl, perhaps a year and a half younger, approached them. In the way of many three-year-olds, in the way of Maia at the same age, this girl stood much too close. She tried to grab the floatie away. She tried, repeatedly, to sit on it. She wedged herself between Maia and her friend and would not leave. She tugged at their bathing suits. All the while, her mother sat nearby, saying nothing.

Maia "used her words." "Please. We're playing. It bothers me when you stand so close." The child ignored her. "Don't! It's my floatie!" Still, the child wouldn't go.

Finally I intervened, suggesting that maybe the other girl would co-operate better if she were given a turn. Reluctantly at first, but with increasing good grace, Maia and Emmie agreed. "Go ahead. You can play with it for ten minutes. Then it's our turn again."

But once the toy was hers, the girl no longer wanted it. It drifted to the pool's perimeter as, with a fixed and slightly manic smile, she chased my daughter and her friend around and around.

At last Maia lost her temper. "We want to play on our own! Go away!" Not that it helped. I had her serve a time-out for rudeness, and then another when she made as if to push the other child. And then another time-out and another, until she had lost a good portion of her precious play time. She fulfilled her time-outs with uncharacteristic forbearance, but I wondered if inside she might be feeling the way I sometimes feel in her presence, worn out by the relentlessness of her claims. What I felt now, though, was angry on her behalf. My friend and I cast hostile glances at the mother, whose only comment on the entire drama, issued with a sniff and an injured pout, was, "Those are not nice girls. Find some nice children to play with."

Suddenly, I remembered that I had seen this pair before, over a year earlier. The child, then a toddler, was playing, or rather teetering, on the ledges of park equipment far too big and dangerous for her, refusing to get out of the way when older children wanted to use the slides. After asking her to move a couple of times and failing to get a response, Maia simply ducked and wriggled past her. The child wailed, and the mother, until then nowhere in evidence, sprang into action, snatching her daughter away and muttering something about Maia's rudeness and my irresponsibility.

"Oh, for heaven's sake," I said. It had been a long day and this park outing was the closest I was going to get to a moment of relaxation. "Just wait until yours is three."

The woman began screaming at me then. "No wonder your daughter has such awful social skills, with you as her model! You're a terrible parent!"

It's true, I thought—though I knew, too, that the woman wasn't entirely in her right mind. No wonder her kid seemed a little "off." Who wouldn't, with a banshee like that for a mother?

Now, though, watching them again at the sun-dappled pool, it occurred to me that I might have confused the causal relationship. Because living with that child would surely drive anybody crazy.

It isn't always difficult. Whole hours, days, weeks, and even months can pass when parenting Maia feels almost like parenting any other spirited and strong-willed child. And what a joy that is. During a recent car ride, she became, for half an hour or so, her healthiest self. On the surface, nothing had changed: she was chattering, nattering, and singing as incessantly and loudly as always. Her energy level was high, and most adults would probably have considered her behaviour annoying. Yet something felt different. Something prompted Mark and me to turn to one another at the same moment, to touch one another and smile. For once, she isn't talking *at* us, I thought. For once, she isn't covertly demanding; it's enough for her to be inside her own skin. I could not believe the gift of peace this brought to me, the way I felt my head clear out and my heart expand in my chest.

No child could be more rewarding to a parent than Maia when she is thriving. She is intelligent, imaginative, active, affectionate, funny, and fun. She works hard, plays hard, and fills our lives with gusto. She is also perfectly suited to be our daughter. Her passions couldn't be more similar to ours. Particularly her love of words. Her vocabulary surpasses that of some children twice her age. "I feel vulnerable," she told an adult dinner guest of ours as they walked together down a darkened hallway. "Oh, really?" said our friend. "And what does vulnerable mean?" "It means you are afraid that you aren't strong enough and that something might hurt you," Maia replied. Every night she asks me to define another word; if she hears the definition once, the word is hers. And it isn't only meaning she responds to. I have seen her shiver with pleasure at a rhyme or a new phrase. I have heard her repeat it to herself again and again, just for delight in the sounds. Hers is a poet's sensibility. I did not make her this way. She just *is*.

"Family fit" is the phrase used by adoption professionals. "There must be family fit." But our problems are not due to an absence of mystical "fit." I cannot imagine feeling closer, more akin, to any child. For better or for worse, I am Maia's mother. And she is my daughter.

When I was Maia's age, my mother and I had an intense and at times combative relationship. I recall one period in particular, when we had just moved to an arid suburb, where our house was the very first one built in a new development. In the mornings, my father drove off to work in our VW Beetle, leaving us without a car and my mother without adult companionship. All around us stretched muddy lots and vacant skies. The nearest people lived miles away; the nearest stores were farther. Mum must have gone crazy, stuck alone there with a chatty three-year-old, day after endless day. She watched the soap operas and ironed my father's shirts and the family's sheets, keeping them damp and rolled in the freezer until she was ready to begin the job. I squatted in front of her on the carpet, sometimes getting tangled in the iron's cord, often begging her to play with me or whining that I was bored. Once in a while she lost her temper and slapped me or called me a brat. A selfish brat. "I hate you," I shrieked back at her. "You're an awful mummy!"

These days, Maia has taken to wailing ' You don't love me!" whenever her father or I tell her to stop doing something, or ask her to do something that she does not want to do. Sometimes she adds, "I don't love you!" This is painful to hear—but all part of the "normal" mother-daughter relationship, and all, to me, expected.

What I didn't expect was having to learn a safe-restraint technique before my child reached the age of five. What I didn't expect was having to bear bruises and bite marks on my arms for weeks, once, just for issuing a time-out. What I didn't expect was to turn around one morning as I was preparing her school lunch and find her pointing a knife at my back. A child's dull-bladed knife, true. But a knife.

At last I find an image of "mothering" that resonates for me. It's a photo that Mark took in the summer. Maia and I had just finished playing dress-up—one of the "floor time" sessions that I build in as part of my therapeutic parenting role. These are one-to-one play periods when Maia directs all the action. Theory holds that allowing children a strong measure of control in their fantasy play will encourage them to relax control in other areas of their lives.

In the photo, Maia and I are still in costume. We sit together on the carpet. She's cuddled in my lap, with my arms around her. In her own lap she cradles her beloved blanket—the "transitional object" that some of the Drs. Doolittle see as a sign that she has internalized my love, and others think ought to be wrested away from her, as a hindrance to the purity of our attachment. Maia smiles sweetly at the camera; she makes a demure and delightful Bo Peep. I, on the other hand, sport the livid green hair and the pointed black hat of the wicked witch.

Maia hates it when I am sad. Sometimes she gets angry and orders me to stop crying; if especially stressed, she might even hit me. But sometimes, instead, she tries to take care of me. "See, Mum?" she says, pulling a funny face, or quoting a silly riddle. "I can make you smile. Don't cry. Please don't cry."

"Boundary issues," my therapist says. "She doesn't know where you stop and she begins."

I'm not sure that I know where I stop and she begins, either. Musing about that photo of Maia and me, I wonder why I've chosen it. Because consider this: in the picture, the child is sweet and innocent and all good. But who or what is the mother? Is she the competent, playful and smiling one who holds the child and contains the child? Or is she really the mean witch with mustard teeth?

And as if that were not confusing enough—look again. Mummy is wearing a nametag, the kind that parents and tots are asked to put on whenever they participate in some semi-organized activity at the gym or the local library. Look; look closely. The name on this tag is not the mother's. It is the child's.

I do my best. I try to be the strong, all-loving parent that she needs. But a poor night's sleep, a skipped meal, or an annoying phone solicitation can cut my patience short; a death in the family, a conflict with a friend, or trouble in my work can draw me inward, away from her demands. "Mum, Mum, Mum, Mum, Mum," she shouts. Often, in her presence, my pulse begins to race, my breathing tightens and my neck cramps. Her anxiety becomes my own. Vicarious trauma, this is called. And sometimes the pressure builds too high. She'll be hanging on my pant leg, chasing me into the bathroom, issuing orders in an even bossier tone than usual, or shrieking at me—and I'll explode. 'Go away! Leave me alone. Mum needs a time-out!"

Of course this sends her into a tailspin. Her mother, rejecting her. It is the worst thing she can imagine. Never mind "imagine." She doesn't *need* to imagine; it is the worst thing she has ever lived, and she relives it every time I walk away. Afterwards, I curse myself. I wonder if she will ever recover. I wonder if I will ever recover from the guilt. And I wonder if, at bottom, her ambivalence is nothing more and nothing less than a mirror of my own.

While we're cuddling one afternoon, Maia confides, "The worst day in my life was when they cut my umbilical cord. I wanted to stay inside my birth mother forever.

I was so comfortable in there." A few days later, though, I hear her on her play phone, talking to the birth mother. "You should *not* have left me," she says, with sizzling indignation. "I was only a baby. That was bad of you. You were wrong!"

One night, Maia gives me a good-night kiss that bypasses my cheek and lands smack on my ear, making it buzz and ring. "I think you did that on purpose," I say to her. "What's going on? Why do you try to hurt me when I'm about to leave your room?"

"I don't want you to go," she says. It's simple, and it's obvious, but articulating the idea seems to help her. The next night, instead of hurting me, she bars the door to my exit.

Her rages become less frequent and less violent. She is one of only two in her kindergarten class to have earned three stars for "home reading." She can focus on her drawing for half an hour. Sometimes she remembers to ask before she grabs. At day care, she is making friends. So many signs of progress.

But on our worst days, I still fear that I am raising a sociopath. At minimum, a "borderline."

She will be pregnant, drugged, and on the streets by the age of sixteen.

She will be in jail by the age of twenty.

At thirty, she will ruin some psychiatrist's life with false accusations of sexual improprieties.

At forty, she will wake up alone, with no partner and no child.

She will never really learn how to love.

She will never really love me.

Every night she wakes. Sometimes shrieking with fear; sometimes bellowing in rage. But tonight, she comes on quiet feet and stands silently next to our bed. I wake up and follow her back to her room. If she crawled in with us, Mark's sleep would be disturbed too; this way, at least two of us will get some rest. Three years ago, that would not have been true. Back then, she was made so anxious by the intimate presence of another that she would stay awake all night and keep us awake, too—jumping, hitting, rolling, pulling hair. I count it as one of my incontrovertible victories over her past that now, when sharing a bed with one of us, she returns to sleep within minutes.

Under the canopy of her double bunk bed I feel a double layer of darkness. We settle in. When she was younger and still struggling with pronoun usage, she would have barked, "Put your arm around you. Put my arm around me!" when she wanted to be held. Those pesky boundary issues, again. Now, instead, she gently but firmly grasps my arm and wraps it around herself, tucking it in just so. I brush her fine hair away from my chin, adjust my hand so it won't get pins and needles, inhale the scent of her apricot shampoo.

An hour or so later she cries out, thrashing and kicking and whining. She grinds her teeth with a sound like a rake on cement. A night terror or a bad dream.

"Shhh, It's all right," I whisper, my promise to her a kind of prayer. "Everything will be all right. Mummy loves you. Mummy loves you."

Rolling closer, she fishes for my leg with her foot and snuggles against me. She finds my arm and drapes it across herself once more. I don't know what tomorrow will bring—whether she'll bend flexibly with the day's demands and look at me with love in her eyes, or whether she will harden herself to shield her wounds, and blindly, helplessly hurt me. But for now, her breathing calms and slows, slows and calms. She pulls me close. She does not push me away.

Mind Reader

In the nineteenth century, if you wanted to understand yourself better, you went to a phrenologist and had your head examined. Phrenologists argued that each human faculty corresponded to a particular "organ" of the brain and that the shape and size of these organs suggested their relative power. They massaged their subjects' skulls, feeling for the bumps, and then massaged their egos, telling them about their characters. Queen Victoria believed in phrenology; so did Whitman and Dickens and Charlotte Brontë and George Eliot. Ambrose Bierce did not. He called it "the science of picking the pocket through the scalp. It consists in locating and exploiting the organ that one is a dupe with."

Today, if you want your head or, more likely, somebody else's head examined, you go to a psychoneurophysiologist. I went to one not long ago. Desperate, determined, undeterred by cost or lack of insurance coverage, undismayed by the doubts of conventional physicians, undaunted by the practitioner's Dickensian-sounding name, I switched off my cell phone at the threshold of Dr. Swingle's office and carried my daughter across.

Cell phones interfere with the equipment. Unlike phrenologists, psychoneurophysiologists put faith in technology, so for contemporary patients the grip of bare fingers has given way to the tickle of electrodes—metal discs shaped like the suction cups on the ends of plastic darts. But we didn't see those right away. I saw a wall of books and four or five computers. Maia saw three large swivel chairs. She dove for the biggest of these, the one behind Dr. Swingle's desk, and began to spin. He regarded her calmly. I sat down in one of the other chairs and stared out the windows at the North Shore mountains. Coffee sloshed out of my cup onto the doctor's rug. He didn't flinch. Grey-bearded, grey-eyed, and bespectacled, his countenance wouldn't have seemed out of place in a Victorian parlour.

I gave him her medical and developmental history—the long litany of concerns that had brought us to his door—but Dr. Swingle waved the papers aside without even looking at them. Instead, he ushered Maia toward a computer screen on the other side of the room and told her to put her feet on the stool below. Then he fixed a couple of delicate wires to her ears with tiny alligator clips. "Ouch," she said. "I'm not going to wear earrings when I grow up."

An electroencephalograph measures and tracks electrical activity in the brain. The five electrodes that Dr. Swingle now placed at different places on Maia's skull—swabbing them first with a conductive gel that she said felt cold—would transform the electrical activity inside her head into patterns, called brainwaves. "Watch the screen," he instructed her. "Stay perfectly still, and watch the bars."

Moving to the computer next to hers, he pushed a button. On his monitor, columns of numbers appeared; on hers, rectangles of red, blue, and yellow danced erratically, like the keys of a player piano. The blue bar predominated. After a few minutes he adjusted one of the electrodes and started a new test; the coloured bars moved differently this time, more red than blue. "Nice and still," he repeated. "Now I need you to close your eyes. Okay. You can open them again. You're doing very well."

The brainwaves have names like fraternities—theta, alpha, beta, delta, gamma—and, like frat boys, they squabble for supremacy. Delta is a very slow wave, up to four Hz, seen most commonly in deep sleep and very young children. Theta waves are associated with reverie and déjà vu; it's normal for them to increase during adolescence. Alpha waves, at 8.5 to 12 Hz, are characteristic of a relaxed, alert state of consciousness, while beta waves increase during periods of active or anxious thinking.

Something on the shelf above her head caught Maia's eye. "Is it just me," she said, "Or is that a real *skull?*" I came over to take a closer look. The jaw was ordinary bone-colour. The top was painted grey and sectioned off with white lines, then over-painted in bright primary hues like the ones on her computer monitor. "Eeew," she squealed. "It *is* real, isn't it?" Dr. Swingle moved the electrodes again. "Mum," Maia moaned. "It's *looking* at me."

The electroencephalograph is generally accepted as a useful tool in the diagnosis of brain injury, stroke, and epilepsy. Whether it has wider application to the diagnosis of so-called "soft" neurological problems and psychological or behavioural disorders is more controversial. But according to neuropsychologists like Dr. Swingle, anomalous patterns of activity in the different regions of the brain correspond with specific mental, emotional, or learning disorders. Every brainwave pattern paints a particular picture and every picture tells a story. Too much theta in relation to beta in the frontal lobes often signals ADHD. Fast alpha frequencies go along with anxiety and hyper-vigilance. Low-voltage slow activity correlates to dementia; alpha asymmetry in the frontal regions indicates depression. Neuropsychologists also believe they can treat these problems with neurotherapy, a kind of biofeedback for the brain—but this remains an alternative approach.

Maia sighed. Dr. Swingle fiddled with his dials. I looked around. Besides the skull, the shelf supported an odd assortment of objects, including a robotic car, a soapstone sculpture of a fish, a globe, and a monkey-like mask. On the walls hung some professional degrees, along with several drawings of the brain—among them, I was startled to notice, a nineteenth-century etching taken from a phrenology text. The doctor apparently has a sense of humour.

A wiggle break and a few more rounds. Then Dr. Swingle sent Maia to the "treasure chest" in the waiting room. He stared at the printout in his hand. "Here," he said, and he pointed to an outline of the brain, "These numbers imply trauma." He shrugged, palms up, waiting for my response. I nodded. "And here," he continued, "too much theta. This is the hyperactivity people associate with ADHD. But it's minor. In the ballpark I play in, she barely makes the field." There was more. Extreme stubbornness. A tendency to perseverate. Lapses of short-term memory, attachment disorder, inability to read social cues, emotional reactivity, tantrums, explosions. One by one he read the ratios, divining my daughter more quickly, more accurately than any professional I'd yet encountered.

173

She came back into the room. "I got a rock," she announced.

Dr. Swingle picked it up and held it to the light. "Ah," he said. "Chalcedony. An agate. Soothes the mind and promotes balance. Alleviates hostilities, quiets thunder and lightning." He handed it back to Maia. "You'd best hang on to that."

The Easy Way

Here's how it happens. I'm at the park, surrounded by other mothers, all of us pushing our preschoolers on the swings or watching them swarm around the sand pile. One woman is pregnant and another asks when she's due.

"Last week of August. But earlier than that, if I have any say. My mom's coming to help and she can only stay until the first week of September."

A crack of laughter. "Nice try, but you'll be late. You were late last time."

The pregnant one rubs her belly and hums. From above, the rustle of leaves and the scrabble of squirrels leaping from branch to branch. Our voices rise and fall in a comfortable rhythm, interrupted by occasional shouts from the children or pleas for a snack. Eventually, talk turns to labour. Whose was longest, hardest, who had an epidural or an episiotomy, how long it took the scar from that C-section to heal. Somebody leaves to make sure her son gets his nap at the necessary hour. Someone else looks for a quiet bench where she can nurse. Cradling her baby, she offers her breast and his crying stops. The two of them sit locked in a trance of semi-erotic torpor, temporarily lost to the rest of us, gone to a private world.

As long as we're comparing developmental milestones or talking about the best places to find shoes for toddler feet, I chatter along with the rest. But when the subject turns to pregnancy and labour, I'm quiet. At the mention of morning sickness, I distract myself with the thought of a spicy sauce I'll make for the evening's pasta and the Chardonnay cooling in our fridge. At a glimpse of stretch marks, I look away. I stare through and past the others, seeking a place to fix my gaze, any place but the Madonna and child beneath the maples. Mostly, my silence goes unnoticed. I'm happy to keep it that way. But every once in a while one of the park mothers will ask a question that forces me to out myself. A question like, "Who's your obstetrician?" Or, "Ever consider a home birth?" Then, stepping back, fanning my fingers in a gesture that denies authority and feels like an abdication, I answer. "I'm no expert."

"Oh. Right. I forgot." My questioner's face brightens. Released momentarily from the mental fog induced by parenting two kids, both in diapers, she adds, "You did it the easy way."

It must have been easy for Mark to produce that sperm sample—shut but not locked (there was no lock) in a dingy hospital supply room, interrupted—"Oh! Excuse me!"—by a nurse in search of an extra bedpan. I know it got easy for me to inject myself with Pergonal; after a couple of cycles, I was such a pro I could take it with me when we went to a dinner party and do it in the powder room; I'd be back before our hosts had finished pouring the wine.

Pumped full of hormones, I released extra eggs, and doubled or tripled our chances every cycle. But when I was assured that my eggs were like those of a "much younger woman," I didn't know whether to feel flattered or insulted. Mark, for his part, made quantities of excellent sperm; strangely, although he is a decade and a half older than me, no one implied that it might be stale-dated.

Early mornings on insemination days, we'd pass the precious liquid through a sliding door at the hospital; later, purified and intensified, it would enter me through the ministrations of one of several doctors who prowled the ward. Some were gentler and more capable than others. After my injection, I'd wait for half an hour, knees akimbo under a thin blue sheet. Gazing across the frozen lake at the U.S. border, I'd wonder when the ice might begin to crack, hoping for an omen.

Once I was a couple of days late. That's the closest we got. When the clinic closed for the summer we decided to stop. We knew it wasn't going to work. We knew we didn't want to go on to in vitro fertilization or the fancier and costlier technologies. Some people engage in what are aptly called the "fertility wars" for a decade or more, spending sums that rival the defence budgets of small developing nations. But our approach came closer to old-fashioned trench warfare. A long period of waiting and watching followed by a short and desperate volley; then retreat on one front—and surprise advance on another.

Our decision to adopt was instant and mutual. You might even call it easy. Walking back from the hospital 177 after that last insemination, we stopped, looked at each other, and said, "Let's do it." Our faces stretched into smiles. We hadn't been planning this. I was already a step-parent to Mark's older kids and he was already a parent; we'd wanted a child *together* and didn't think adoption could fulfill that dream. And then, at precisely the same moment, we understood that it could. Our child would not be biologically related to us, but she'd be no less the child of our love for that. As a couple, as a family, we'd always prized what made us atypical. Multi-generational, multi-national, multi-ethnic, multi-linguistic. Mark and his older kids and I followed different religious traditions; we favoured different aesthetics; we subscribed to different politics. We argued passionately, listened attentively, changed our minds—or didn't. Summers found us in the kitchen cooking kosher for Mark's eldest son, meat-and-potatoes for another son—until he turned vegetarian—and vegan for their sister. This is what we loved about one another. Our differences, and our willingness to respect and learn from those differences. *Needs more garlic! Pass the lemon. Where's the pepper?* This is what we shared—delight in strong, distinctive flavours. Looked at that way, adding to our family through an inter-country adoption seemed like the deepest possible expression of our values.

Calling the social worker was a cinch. Josie was the only one in our city's phone directory licensed to perform adoption home studies. Plump and panting with the exertion of climbing the six steps to our front door, she collapsed onto our couch and presented us with a stack of questionnaires designed to test our fitness to parent. *Some people believe that adoptive parents are desperate for a child. What is your level of desperation? Did your parents agree on discipline? Who handled most of it? What tactics did they use? How do you handle conflict? What about you is difficult to relate to?* Our answers took months to compile and made a mountain. Then came health checks, police checks, financial checks, immunizations, passport renewals, visas, and multiple letters of reference for each of us from family, friends, and co-workers.

Meanwhile, chins and grey pin curls wobbling, Josie mounted yet another set of stairs to the prospective nursery, wheezing out warnings about childproofing as she went. We counted ourselves lucky; at least she hadn't run a white-gloved finger across our mantel. Satisfied at last that two teachers who had already been raising children together for the better part of a decade would make responsible parents, she condensed her findings into a report and mailed it to the provincial government, where a recent hireling, flexing puny muscles, wanted to know why Mark hadn't worked harder to save his first marriage. Hadn't worked harder? Twenty years of family therapy, individual therapy, couples therapy and an attempt at reconciliation hadn't been enough? Even Josie thought this was going too far. By then, we'd been trying for five years to have a baby. It was six months since we'd begun the adoption process. We knew we had at least a year of waiting ahead of us. Add another month to that wait.

We took out a loan to pay for the adoption. We got married to qualify for the adoption, although until then we'd been comfortably, consciously unwed. Like most parents-to-be, we studied child development, but unlike most, we broke from Dr. Spock and Penelope Leach to brush up on Chinese history. We listened to and countered objections from friends who considered inter-country adoption immoral. We educated ourselves about potential challenges the newest member of our family might face, challenges to do with adoption itself, with loss of culture, with minority status. We even decorated that nursery and put together a crib. ABC, easy as 123.

Actually, it was. After the uncertainty, the grief, and the loss of control we'd felt over infertility, adoption offered a clear process with a known result. We'd complete our paperwork, send it to our agency, wait for a phone call, and when the call finally came, we'd cram formula, bottles, blankets, rattles, baby clothes, weeks' worth of diapers, gifts, orphanage donations, and a *Rough Guide* to China into two small suitcases and fly to Beijing and from there to another as-yet-unknown Chinese city, where a stranger would introduce us— sleep-deprived, jet-lagged and disoriented—to the equally travel-weary and disoriented baby who would become our daughter. We'd stamp our fingers and her feet in red ink to formalize our relationship, strap her into a Snuggli, and for the next two weeks we would cart her in the forty-degree heat to the principal tourist sites of her native land, a land whose language and customs and currency would be alien to us—though surely less alien than we—big-nosed, cheese-stinking, nonsense-talking *wai guo ren*, foreigners—would seem to her. At last, touring over and acquaintanceship established, we'd board a plane for a thirteen-hour trans-Pacific flight, usher our baby through customs, fill out another stack of forms to make her a Canadian citizen, fly another five hours, take her home, and love her. What could be easier than that?

Friends have described their first ultrasounds to me. I've seen the images. Tiny amphibians, swimming in their amniotic seas, fists like sailor's knots or fingers splayed like starfish. "It's the first time he seemed real," one friend mused, "even though he looked like an extra-terrestrial."

What's eerie about these photos is how early they're available. On the outside, you don't even show. On the inside, a *being*, complete with head, shoulders, knees and toes—and here is proof. Adoptive parents wait longer for this confirmation. We got ours—called the "referral photo"—only six weeks before we travelled to meet our daughter. In the picture, she was three months old. She did not look like an extraterrestrial. She looked like a porcelain doll, or a starlet, if you ignored the chrome bars of the crib in the background. Orphanage staff had laid her on a red blanket. Her right arm emerged from the folds of her yellow sweater, aimed toward the viewer in a wave. Or maybe a punch. She was tiny, delicate-featured, with expressive feet, a sad mouth, and a direct even accusing stare. We thought she was the most beautiful baby we'd ever seen.

Meeting her was a shock. She seemed so different from that picture. And, unlike most of the other babies adopted in our travel group, she didn't cry. I was not fool enough to read this as a positive sign. In my arms, those first few moments, Maia reached to explore, but anxiety fuelled her exploration. She heard everything, watched everything, her plump cheeks indrawn in an expression of soundless worry. Later, in our hotel room, she sat for hours making that strange face, and when the effort of maintaining her vigilance became too great, she lost all muscle tone and slumped toward the carpet, a cooked noodle. Even then, she fought sleep. She plucked at her own skin, scratched her ears raw in an effort to keep alert. When she finally dropped off, she screamed out every hour or two and made that rake-on-cement noise. I stared at her, trying to figure out the source of the sound. "She only has two teeth," I said to Mark. Until then I had not known that a person could grind her jawbones.

How could I mother this child?

A few days into her life with us, she woke with a laugh and pulled herself up on her crib rail. *Look at me,* she seemed to say. *Look at who I really am!* Not the withdrawn and terrified creature we'd known until then, but a vibrant, curious, and determined toddler. Once in Canada, she quickly thrived, walking and talking on schedule, exploring her world with delight. An English-born acquaintance once commented that she looked "chuffed," watching the world from her sleigh on winter afternoons that first year with us. So she did. She looked chuffed a lot of the time. Still, months after her arrival from China, while sitting in her highchair after a meal or watching the dance of green leaves beyond a window, she would sometimes fall silent. Her body would begin to shake, a small current passing through her so she trembled, seemingly in sympathy with the leaves outside, and then with greater agitation, like an electric toothbrush. Were these seizures? Traumatic flashbacks? There was so much I didn't know. Couldn't know.

"Couldn't you have kids of your own?" people used to say to me. Assuming, of course, that adoption, as a second choice, must be second best. Our culture, like most others, begins in the procreational imperative. To adopt a child, especially one who cannot be passed off as "one's own," is to insist that family can be bound by invisible threads of love as surely as by chains of genes. And this remains a radical claim in our society. The idea that blood is thicker than water, that biological relationship trumps all, dies hard.

Adoptive parents may come reluctantly to the revolution, but invariably we make good fighters for the cause. Like most, I bristled self-righteously at the suggestion that adoption was an inferior way to form a family. I promulgated "adoption-positive" language. Say "birth-mother," not "real mother" or "natural mother." Say "relinquished" or "placed for adoption," not "aban-

182

doned" or "given away" or "unwanted." Say "was
adopted," not "is adopted." And never, never, never ask
how much the baby cost! The unflattering truth is that
I may have committed these and other adoption-
unfriendly *faux pas* myself, before I became part of what
the social workers call "the adoption triad." It would be
tough *not* to imbibe some of our culture's negative attitudes towards adoption.

183

Those who don't disparage adoption tend to idealize
it. The first time someone joked that I'd done it "the
easy way" I felt stung by the tactlessness of the remark.
But later, I understood the comment as a backhanded
way of welcoming me to the club. I may have escaped
the pains of childbirth but not the sticky joys of parenthood itself. "Once you have her," friends said, "you'll feel
exactly the same as any other mother." They meant to
support, to console, to reassure. And oh—how badly I
wanted to believe them.

What made Mark and me agree so readily to adopt?
The answer's easy. We'd simply traded one stereotype for
another. We may have prided ourselves on the ways we
were atypical, but when it came to ideas about adoption,
we weren't all that different from anybody else. Once,
adoption had scared us because, like most couples, we
had wanted a child of "our own." Later, adoption had
presented itself as a magical solution, a promise of
"happily ever after." Now, we brought our baby home
and found, not our perfect fantasy child, but a real
person with needs and strengths and weaknesses of her
own. And we faced a welter of unanticipated questions,

a thicket of unexpected problems. Here, too, we were no different from most parents, but the extent of Maia's needs and their unfamiliarity walloped us, sent us reeling. And the exhaustive home study that in theory should have prepared us proved completely irrelevant to the challenges we actually faced.

When you adopt, there is no way you can analogize Matthew's dyslexia to your Uncle Bill's, no way you can compare Emma's stubborn streak to your own. So you tend to read every twitch and tantrum for darker messages. What if your child grows up to be the next Charles Manson—wasn't he adopted? And when you adopt a child who has been living in an institution, you pledge your life to someone who may be medically, nutritionally, and emotionally deprived, someone who has no concept of family, someone who may never have heard the word for mother in any language. Nobody talked or hummed to *this* baby in the womb. Or if they did, you might not want to know what they said.

Think adoption is easy? Push your pre-schooler on the swings while, nearby, another mother nurses, the infant making a pillow of her body. Then imagine your own child, locked in a noisy orphanage, a bottle propped against her lips but whisked away before she's finished drinking. See that mother changing her baby? Think of your own baby, strapped to a potty seat for hours at a time, scarred from the restraints. Hear that toddler chortle as he reaches for his new toy, listen as he lisps in clever syllables. Remember the blank look in your daughter's eyes when you first met, and the back of her head, flattened from ten months' pressure against a crib's thin mattress. Carry her everywhere; celebrate with sparkling wine the day she first learns how to grip with her legs and no longer feels like dead weight against your body. Rub her back through her night terrors, hold her as she rages, try not to wince when she hits or bites. Try not to wince when she tells you her birth mother would be nicer to her. Wonder if you and she will ever enjoy the easy trust that develops when needs are properly met from the start. Easy, peasy, lemon squeezy.

Media representations of celebrity adoptions— Sharon Stone and Mia Farrow and Angelina Jolie collecting babies like extra pairs of shoes—may make adoptive motherhood look like the ultimate self-indulgence. But that's not how it really is, not even for them. Becoming a mother—any mother—means learning to see through your child's eyes, to feel with your child's heart. Becoming an adoptive mother means accepting from the start that your child's heart beats to another body's rhythm.

Does that mean the disparagers are right? Is adoption second best?

I don't think so.

Imagine you're learning to dance. You begin without the warm-up and you miss the first few classes, so you and your new partner are clumsy. You tire easily, lose confidence, lurch and tread on one another's toes; sometimes you even fall. The steps you're learning are different—more intricate than the ones the other dancers need to learn, so while your classmates dip and swing, you'll still be practising your basic moves. Sometimes you'll envy them, wishing you had it as easy; ironically, a few of them may envy you because you got to skip those dull introductory lessons.

Never mind. Keep dancing. You'll need to improvise a lot of the choreography. After all, unlike most of the others, you're combining moves from more than one dance form and more than one tradition. But improvisation is freeing, and drawing on multiple sources adds texture and richness to your art.

As you gain grace, you'll glow with pride at your own achievement. Because you're unusual, you may attract stares in public and the kind of attention that nobody wants; yet in time, you'll move so fluidly that people will comment on how miraculously you're matched. By then, like most dancers, you'll have lost your self-consciousness, forgotten the pain and embarrassment of your first halting steps. By then, you'll wonder what gave your life meaning before you learned to dance.

Friends of mine say that they find it hard to remember who they were before they became mothers. For me, that's easy. All I have to do is re-read the letters of reference I got for our adoption. *Loving, honest, loyal, nurturing, respectful of others. Never shies from challenges. An avid reader, direct communicator, passionately curious, intellectually agile. Has a fine sense of the ridiculous.*

Speaking of ridiculous, who ever heard of an unflattering letter of reference?

But my friends were, if anything, more forthright than most. Along with the panegyrics they permitted themselves a few little words like *impatient* and *intense*. I recognize myself more easily today in those labels than in the glowing ones.

I ask Mark for his perspective. He's lived with me a long time; he ought to know. How has becoming a mother changed me? "You're more patient," he says. "And less. More patient with Maia. And less patient with the world."

So I am. Bored sometimes beyond reckoning, still I can play with her for hours; ten minutes into a mildly predictable movie, I jump from our couch, saying I have better things to do than watch that crap. Nine times out of ten, I swallow my anger with her when I feel like exploding. Nine times out of ten, I speak my anger—or, more shamefully, shout it—if provoked by anyone else.

Yet in a strange way, my vices have become virtues. She needs that endurance and that fierceness from me. Parenting a young child has a way of focusing any woman's attention. Parenting an adopted, traumatized child has a way of concentrating that focus to a laser's force.

"She's got a good head," my father says. "She's quick! She likes her vegetables. Such a pretty smile." Nothing but compliments, even though keen eyes like his can't fail to see that sometimes she can't sit still, that she tantrums long after other kids her age have stopped. My mother makes her red jello and indulges her with too much TV.

When she hears from me how stubborn Maia is, she does not tell me that I'm getting a taste of my own medicine. When she hears about night terrors and night wakings, she doesn't tell me what to do. She does think I'm mistaken to imagine that Maia's early history has anything to do with present difficulties. "She can't remember," she says from time to time. But mostly she doesn't argue. She listens.

My parents, unlike my peers at the park, have lived long enough to learn a simple truth. Parenting is never easy. Skip one kind of trouble and you'll get another. If it's not premature birth, it's colic. If it's not a lack of friends at school, it's too many. If it's not shyness to the point of withdrawal, it's rudeness and disrespect. The thing you most dreamed of sharing with your child is the thing she cannot do. The quality that most irritates you in others is the one your child shows to excess. And even perfect children get hurt or sick and die too young. The only thing you can do with a child is love her as well as you can, for as long as you can, hoping that your flawed and broken love will sustain her.

Late afternoon. The schoolyard is nearly deserted. Just me and Maia, now six, and two older girls. Grade Twos. Maia has warned me about them. Catherine and Jennica. One a Barbie-doll blonde, the other a tough-looking Asian. They like to "budge" in line—especially when adults aren't watching.

So I stand about fifteen feet away and watch.

When it's Maia's turn on the rings, the other girls stare at me. They whisper. One jabs the other with her elbow. They stare again.

I can guess what's coming. It won't be the first time.

Finally, the dark-haired one, Jennica, calls out. "Are you her mother?"

Maia reaches for the rings. Her face, already taut with concentration, tightens a fraction more.

"Yes, I'm her mother."

Usually it ends here, but these kids are bold. More whispering, this time louder, and the blonde girl giggles. "No. I mean, are you *really* her mother. Was she *born* from you?"

Maia grasps the bar, drops, and swings. If you didn't know her, you might think she hadn't heard the question. But I know she has heard, and I know she is hurting. Later, she'll tell me that kids do this all the time—ask her why she looks different than me, ask about her *real* mom—and she hates it. It makes her feel singled out. "Like a freak." Later still, I'll make up a rhyme to remind her that difference signifies strength as well as weakness, and we'll laugh together as we chant: *I'm not a freak; I'm unique!* But now, something wild and wildly protective leaps up in me. I think about her first steps, her first English words, the way she takes my hand in her own small, calloused one when we walk across a busy street. I think of the way she looked at me, those first few days in China, with a gaze so penetrating and intent that I feel as if I haven't blinked since—nor will I, until I sense she is ready to look away. And forgetting for a moment that these two girls are children, I want to shout at them, to shame them. No—I'll be honest. *Remembering* that they're children, I want to shame them. In my mind, I roar like the Red Queen. *Off with her head!* Or dredge up disdainful phrases from another era. *How dare you ask a personal question like that, young lady?*

But this is Vancouver, an affluent west-side neighbour-hood where children are coddled and treated like digni-taries, and I'd probably be run off the block for talking that way. Besides, what example would it set for Maia? As she grows up and goes out into the world alone, she'll need to field these questions again and again—whether they're spoken aloud or not. Encountering strangers on the street or at the market, bringing home friends from high school, arriving from college with a new love, she won't have me to shelter her. She'll have to do the explaining. Already, she has had to ask her Mandarin teachers for homework instructions in English: *My mum can't read Chinese.* Soon, she'll be adding, *Did I mention that my parents are white?* And, *This is my brother. No, not my uncle. My brother. I know he's the same age as your dad, but my dad's older.* And in case that weren't enough: *What do you mean you weren't expecting me to look the way I do when you heard my name? Yeah, I'm Chinese. But I'm also part Jewish!* This is her future, and I want to make sure she has the self-acceptance and confidence to negotiate these conversations with dignity and poise.

At the same time, I'm loath to lie. Maybe it's the fault of those reference letters. After all, I have a reputation for honesty to uphold. Ridiculous, I know.

Was she born from you?

On the windowsill of her bedroom, Maia keeps a fish-bowl. In it swim five guppies, golden-brown striped, flecked with teal and red. Gifts from a friend. You'd have thought he'd offered her the world. An animal-lover, forbidden by our landlady from keeping furry pets, she bubbles with love for these bland, cold-blooded creatures, who seem, mysteriously, to have awakened her own maternal impulses. She watches them for hours, feeds them precisely measured doses, helps to clean their bowl every week, reminding me if I lose track of the days. One of these fish is pregnant. Maia has named it Susan. "I know *you* couldn't get pregnant, Mum, but Susan's the best name in the world for a mother."

Are you really her mother?

Eight-year-old girls may be married to literal fact and to logic, but I dive for the heart's truth. Squaring my shoulders, I summon from my teaching days a voice of calm authority. "I'm her mother."

My answer, ambiguous to the two girls, is perfectly clear to Maia. "Forever and ever," she says. She stretches an arm for the next ring, clasps it and swings from side to side, trying to work up the momentum to skip one in the series—a long-time goal of hers, until now unmet.

Jennica raises an eyebrow. Catherine shrugs. They glance from Maia back to me again, chins mulishly lowered, faces sceptical. I stare back. Extending once more, Maia clutches, secures her grip, swings, and her face unfolds in a brilliant smile. She drops to the platform with a thud, feet spread apart, springy and grounded. "Mum! Mum! I did it!"

And something shifts. Jennica moves to let Maia go past, then reaches out to take her own place on the equipment. "Wow," she says. Her voice loses its prematurely cynical edge. She almost allows herself to smile. "Cool."

"Cool," repeats Catherine, flipping her golden hair. Easy.

Mama's Voices

Play

When Maia was twenty-one months old, I left her for ten days to attend a writers' conference in Vermont. She stayed at home with Mark, who took some time off work. From the moment of her adoption at the age of ten months, Mark had been a full partner in caring for her. True, I prepared her bottles and cuddled her and played with her more often; I planned her days and spent more hours in her company. But if she woke with a cry in the night, Mark went to her as often as I did. As a father of three older children—by then, young adults—he knew how to change a diaper, when to sneak a tickle, where to look for the missing blankie, what to do for an owie, and whom to phone in an emergency. Yes, I was her mother. But her dad was the more experienced parent.

Also in the house with us all that spring and summer was one of Mark's older children, Noah. Early evenings, he'd perch on the steps of our west-facing front porch, a Corona in one hand and a book in the other. Maia followed him there, clad only in a diaper, her skin still damp and smelling of the baby oil we squirted in her bath. She plopped down beside him, grabbing his book with clumsy fingers and losing his place in the text, calling out to every dog that ambled past. Noah taught her how to blow across the beer bottle to produce a sound. From the kitchen where I stood preparing supper, I'd hear first his bass blast and then her fainter, eager echo.

194

Most weekdays while I was away, Maia spent several hours—my writing hours—with her regular babysitter, Sue, just as she would have had I been home. At Sue's, the air smelled like flowers and lemon furniture polish. Sue wore denim overalls and a big silver cuff and silver necklaces and earrings, and on sticky afternoons, from the deep recesses of her freezer, she produced juice pop-sicles, translucent as jewels in the sun. Maia sucked on them and then rolled on the floor with the dogs or splashed in the cool water of the swimming pool, super-vised all the while by the woman who, over the years, had cared for each of Mark's older children in their turn, and many other children besides.

None of that could make up for my absence. A toddler needs her mother. A toddler who has lived in an orphan-age for most of her first year needs her mother even more. Afraid of how our separation might affect Maia, and eager to assuage my own guilt, I planned for my departure with the diligence of a general preparing for battle. I read the experts, most of whom declared that children manage this kind of short separation just fine, with support, and emerge from the experience stronger. I played countless games of hide and seek—*Mama goes away, Mama comes back*—and then we practised—one

whole day apart, one night apart—and I gauged her reaction on my return. I gave her a photo of the two of us,
my high-beam smile turned on her, my arms protectively
curved round her body. I searched the library for kids'
stories about mothers who travel for work. I gave her an
old red plaid shirt of mine and watched as she sniffed it
and claimed it. And I gave her a basket of gifts—one for
each night I'd be gone, a tangible calendar—each
present wrapped in brightly coloured tissue and all of
them placed in a big basket. She still has some of those
toys. A plastic tea set. A clock with hands that move, for
teaching time. And the biggest gift, the most extrava-
gant—a Little Tykes tape recorder.

Mark set up the machine that first night and turned it
on. Maia watched, solemn and apprehensive, as the
homemade recording crackled and hissed. Then she
smiled. "Who's that?" Mark asked. "Mama!" she crowed,
swaying back and forth in her excitement. "Mama's...
voices!"

Fast Forward

Four years later, I am on my way to the famous conference for a second time. The day of my flight, I meet with
an agent in Toronto. He has read an essay of mine in a literary journal and wants to discuss it with me. He likes the
piece—likes it a lot—and over coffee at an outdoor café,
he asks whether I'd consider expanding it into a book. If
I write that book, he would very much like to see it.

Light hits the green leaves of the vines growing up
around the patio trellis. Light dances over the spoons

the knives, the porcelain cups. I sip my black Americano, savour its bitter brightness.

The encounter is an emerging writer's dream come true. Or, as my instructor at the conference will put it, "The Schwab's Drug Store fantasy."

Stop

"The Schwab's Drug Store fantasy" *is* a fantasy. Lana Turner, said to have bewitched a talent scout with her beauty while sipping a cola at the soda counter there, was actually discovered at the Top Hat Café. The Top Hat sits across the street from Hollywood High School, where Lana, then known as Judy, was an indifferent student. She may have been drinking a Coke, as the legend goes, but more likely she'd skipped out of class to sneak a cigarette.

Play

The tape I made for Maia included nursery rhymes—traditional favourites like Wee Willie Winky and Banbury Cross and Baa Baa Black Sheep, and modern-day versions by Eric Carle and Sandra Boynton. I recorded stories she already knew, like *Goodnight Moon* and *Runaway Bunny*, and stories that were new to her. Maia hadn't warmed to any of the commercially available books about adoption, so I wrote and read onto tape a version of her own story, explaining how she came to be our daughter. I told anecdotes about my childhood and about her grandparents, to strengthen her sense of history and connection to our family. I read Chinese legends, to strengthen her connection to the country and culture of her birth. I read Blake, and Coleridge, and Keats. I read Edward Lear and Lewis Carroll. Words for counsel. Words for encouragement. Words for information and education. Words for the pure, sweet beauty of words.

Fast Forward

In the years between visits to the famous conference, I have written little. Little for publication, that is. Instead, I've filled out dozens of doctors' forms, responded to psychologists' questionnaires, and recounted increasingly bleak descriptions of what my life's become to parent support groups on the Internet. In the years between visits to this conference, my active, delightful toddler has disappeared and been replaced by a raging, resistant, impulsive changeling. It's hard to believe that someone so small could be so violent. She slams glass doors and rattles the lamps. She pokes her fingers into our eyes. She kicks. She bites. She scratches.

I have tried to understand. I have tried to find help and therapy. I have spent a small fortune on parenting books and have tried, fruitlessly, to follow their recommendations. I am getting used to the disdain or pity of strangers. I am getting used to feeling lonely. I've lost friendships over this; people think it's my fault, that I must be doing something wrong; people, understandably, get tired of my complaining.

The essay the agent likes is the story of our struggle. It is dark and ambiguous and does not offer answers, easy or otherwise.

Stop

Lana Turner described her life as "a series of emergencies." That's an understatement. The first emergency was the murder of her father. John "Virgil" Turner gambled at cards. Once, he boasted too loudly about the tricycle he planned to buy for his only daughter with his winnings. His killer took the money and Lana never got her trike. Instead, she and her mother moved to Los Angeles, where a decade later she began her career, eventually appearing in fifty-four movies, as well as performing in radio, on television, and for the theatre. She became one of the highest-paid women in America. Yet for all her outward success, she never garnered much respect for her work, and at least once, depressed over a box-office flop, she attempted suicide. A lifelong alcoholic, she was married eight times to seven different husbands. One marriage was annulled and the rest ended in divorce. Her love affairs with famous men—Tyrone Power, Howard Hughes—were similarly unhappy and short-lived. Inherited Rh-factor complications ruled out the large family she had dreamed of, but she did bear one child, a daughter, who was only saved from death at birth by an immediate blood transfusion.

Fast Forward

Famous names, clever classmates, gold clapboard buildings, wine and cocktails on a wide veranda overlooking stubble fields and the rumpled shoulders of Robert Frost's fabled Green Mountains. This is the conference. Every morning, in a converted, whitewashed barn called the Little Theatre, over a hundred of us gather to hear faculty and fellows talk about the writing life. *Follow your obsessions*, they say. *Write about what matters to you. Write what bothers you, what you can't get your head around. Write what keeps you awake.* Later, in class, we critique one another's efforts and our instructors advise: *Bring authority of significance to your own stories.* Afternoons, we hike in the woods and pastures. New York agents and editors come to call. And every night, the moon ascends over the mountains and two hundred of us leave our rooms in the clapboard dorms and file into the Little Theatre again, and the screen doors swing shut and the lights go down—all except for one light at the podium, like a campfire glowing in darkness. We angle ourselves onto folding chairs, pull our sweaters tighter against the chill, and listen as one after another the authors take the stage, and above the trilling of crickets, above the din of our own minds, their voices rise—whispering, beseeching, correcting, caressing, complaining, explaining, shouting, persuading, teasing, berating, comforting, lying, and laying it on the line—a symphony of sound, resonating to the rafters, leaving enduring echoes, weaving indelible magic.

Play

Every morning, I called home. I woke early, still on toddler-time. Mist veiled the mountains. Dew dampened the hems of my jeans as I crossed the lawn to an old-fashioned phone booth that stood in the field next to the laundry compound. I dialled the number, waited for the ring.

"I love you, Sweet Bean."

"Mama. I went to the park. I throwed a ball. I swam in the pool."

"The pool! Was the water cold?"

"A tiny tiny *tiny* bit cold."

The sound of breathing. In the background, Mark walking past, heavy-heeled on our creaky wood floors. A cupboard door closing. Then, "Mama. Where are you?"

I drew faces on the booth's foggy glass. A smiley face. A puzzled face. A frown. "How's she doing?" I asked each time Mark came on the line.

"She's fine," he assured me. "She's happy. She loves the tapes."

.

Stop

If Lana Turner had hoped for an easy child, her daughter, Cheryl Crane, must have proved a disappointment. Spoiled and sullen-looking in her early photos, Cheryl later became rebellious and unruly. She had her reasons. At ten, she confided that her mother's current husband, Lex Barker, best known for his role as Tarzan, had been sexually abusing her for the past three years. To her credit—considering how desperate she was for male attention and approval—Lana defended her daughter. In a performance worthy of one of her films, she withdrew a gun from a drawer next to her sleeping husband's bed, nudged the muzzle to his ear and said, "Get out."

Four years later, Cheryl assumed the role of avenging female. For some time, Lana had been trying to extricate herself from an abusive relationship with a small-time hoodlum named Johnny Stompanato. Stompanato refused to leave. One night Cheryl overheard them fighting in her mother's room and became frightened. As their voices rose in anger and Stompanato began threatening to cut her mother's face—the family's livelihood— and to hurt her grandmother, she ran to the kitchen and grabbed a carving knife, which happened to be lying on the counter. (*Happened to be lying on the counter?*) Returning upstairs, she begged her mother to open the door. Stompanato stood with his back to her, leaning over her mother, grasping something in his hands—a weapon, Cheryl believed, or so she later said, although in fact he held a bundle of his clothes, still clinging to their hangers. Over her mother's frantic protests, Cheryl lunged and stabbed him.

Fast Forward

One of my obligations as a scholar at this conference is to give a reading in the Little Theatre. I think about reading from the essay about my daughter, and my stomach clenches. That piece is too long, too personal, too difficult to excerpt, too domestic, too dependent on all its parts for a true effect, I tell myself. What I mean is, that piece is too revealing, too raw. Or maybe it's just too real. I scroll through the documents folder on my laptop, looking for something more suitable.

But walking out by the river one afternoon, reflecting on the history of this place, counting the names of writers who've come here in the past—Anne Sexton, Truman Capote, Toni Morrison, May Sarton, Ralph

Ellison—I am overcome by an ideal of literature as life-changing. *Write your obsessions, write what matters to you, write what you can't get your head around.* That's what those writers did. They wrote about sex and madness and death and childhood and loneliness and race and their stories came from their own lives and they didn't play it safe. I'm playing with the thought of a book. When else will I get to test this material on so large an audience? Suddenly, it seems cowardly not to read from this essay, the essay that I might—or might not—expand. After all, what's the worst that could happen? Nobody here knows me. Nobody knows my daughter.

I approach the podium, peer into the lights, pretend to look at an audience that I can't see through the glare. Leaning hard onto the surface of the wood to prevent myself from shaking, I read. And surprise—it's over almost before I know it. Afterwards, I look up from my pages to find myself surrounded. Editors of journals press their cards into my hand, inviting submissions. Faculty members offer congratulations. Days later, participants collar me in the cafeteria line or sidle closer under the shade of those wide verandas. *My son was like that. My wife works with kids like yours. My cousin just adopted a kid like the one you wrote about. My sister-in-law has two daughters like that.* Everyone, it seems, has a similar story. Everyone wants to know more.

I try not to become too inflated with self-regard.

Stop

An exciting new voice. A bold, authentic voice. A stylish, urban voice. A raw, unvarnished voice. A mature voice in full possession of its powers. Loved the voice! Sorry, we didn't like the voice. I've found my voice. I've lost my voice. 203

Fast Forward

With my instructor's permission, I substitute this piece for the one I'd originally submitted, and ask my classmates to consider how it might be expanded, opened up, for a book. I don't know what I expect. Probably more of what happened at the reading. Most of my classmates are working on books themselves. Some of my classmates were in that audience, some were part of the group that later surrounded me. So what happens comes as a rude surprise.

Here are the things my classmates say:

> Hard to say how you could do this; you're still in the
>   middle of it.
> It's not your story. It's your daughter's story.
> You shouldn't write this. It's too risky for your child
> You'll ruin your daughter's life.
> Can't see this as a book.
> It's wrong to write about a child.
> Don't worry. You'll find other subjects.
> If you must write this, put it in a drawer.

Here is what our Teaching Fellow says—(she's a girl; she wears ankle-strap wedgies in dark red kid, the kind that Lana Turner might have worn, and I want a pair):

> *Ethically, this is wrong. It would represent a huge*
> *betrayal.*
> *Writing it would violate confidentiality, and would*
> *irreparably damage your relationship with your*
> *daughter.*

Here is what my Instructor, the famous memoirist, says:

> *Renunciation is also a part of the writing life.*
> *I would worry about you as a person and a writer*
> *if you pushed yourself into the limelight with this*
> *material.*
> *Save yourself as a writer.*

Stop
Lana Turner died in 1995 of throat cancer.

Fast Forward
My Canadian reserve collapses. Tears gush from my eyes, trail down my cheeks, and trickle to my chest. I think of Niagara Falls. More water on *our* side. My classmates pretend they don't notice. They keep on talking, saying again what they've already said. Nobody offers me a break. Nobody offers a tissue. I wipe my face with the back of my bare arm. The woman beside me, a therapist in her regular life, fishes in her bag and retrieves a thin paper napkin, the kind you find on the tabletops of diners in aluminum dispensers, the kind that Lana Turner might have dabbed to her lips when a stranger

approached her in the Top Hat Café with his card. My classmate hands me this napkin before resuming her arguments against my project. Her eyes are soft and brown but something in their expression reminds me of a puppy you might find digging up your garden. The puppy is sorry. But only because it's been caught.

At the midpoint of the workshop, after they are done with me and ready to move on to the next victim, I try to get into the bathroom. But someone has beat me to it, so I spend the next hour piggy-eyed, blotchy, and silent throughout discussion of my classmate's submission. My tears continue to flow. I have never cried this much in public. I can't remember the last time I cried this much, period. Maybe when I was my daughter's age? After class, my humiliation complete, I retreat to my room, where I lie face-down on the bed. Like the schoolgirl I've been reduced to.

Stop

The symptoms of cancer of the throat, or larynx, depend mainly on the size and location of the tumor. Most cancers of the larynx begin on the vocal cords. These tumors are seldom painful, but they almost always cause hoarseness or other changes in the voice.

Fast Forward

I wear sunglasses to my meeting with the instructor. I apologize for crying in class.

"Oh," she says. "No need to apologize. We all come here for professional validation and advancement." She pauses as if to let that sink in. Evidently, validation won't be among the things I pack for my trip home. "I *expected* you to break down," she goes on. "I just wasn't sure when."

Behind my glasses, I blink, grateful for their protection.

"You know," she muses, "your story reminds me a bit of one that I have wanted to write for a long while, about a friend of mine who is a priest...and a pedophile. Nobody wants me to write this story. People don't want to hear that he might not be evil, or that I might want to know him anyway."

She's been wearing sunglasses, too. She takes them off. Her face, round, pale, and unlined, does not betray her age, does not reveal a thing about who she might be. "I haven't written that story," she says. "It makes people uncomfortable."

Stop

I've promised my family that each may pass on the book. I've promised to take out anything that anyone objects to—anything at all....I don't believe in a writer's kicking around people who don't have access to a printing press. They can't defend themselves.

—Annie Dillard

Writers are always selling somebody out.

—Joan Didion

Writing...is like rearing children.

—Annie Dillard

Rewind

Write about what obsesses you. Write what bothers you, what you can't get your head around. Write what keeps you awake.

My daughter is what obsesses me. My daughter keeps
me awake.

Record

Once upon a time there was a writer who could spin words into gold. She was as gentle as she was gifted, and as kind as she was keen, and growing up, she paid close attention to her unusual and unhappy family and to her feelings about them—as most writers do. Her first book, a pellucid autobiographical novel, won the acclaim of critics, the admiration of readers, and the agony and ire of the family members she had drawn upon in creating her "troubled" characters. The writer smiled modestly for the cameras and took her bows in public, winced and grieved and repented in private, and then, like all good writers, she sat down to work on Book Number Two. But before she got far into it, the writer married and bore children, and the children needed nursing and then their noses needed wiping and then they needed clothes and books and college funds, and the writer took a job, because Book Number Two wasn't finished yet and not even the strong sales of her first novel could feed her ravenous family.

Nighttimes, in her attic office, the writer wrote. Having used her family for the first book, she was shy of doing so again. She worried that her work was too purely personal. She worried that she was nothing but a navel-gazer. She wanted to make a difference in the world. But between calls from the school and Halloween treats and dentist appointments and doctor appointments and nightly tuck-ins with her kids, the words came in fits and starts, jerky and then slow—so slow, so cryptic sometimes, that they felt almost like semaphore. So one day, on a tip from a good friend, the writer decided that she needed a change of genres. She would forget about writing stories for a while. She would take her gift for telegraphed images and write for film, write scripts that brought attention to serious political problems, scripts that showed she was more than a mere "domestic" scribbler, more than a navel-gazer.

Sure enough—because she was a good writer, a writer whose touch could turn anything to gold—success followed. Awards, articles in the press, offers of more work. The writer felt happy. She'd produced something that had reached a wide audience—a much wider audience than any literary book could reach. Something that might help others. Still—in the darkness of her office, her desk lamp beaming onto her russet hair, if she was honest with herself she had to admit it: she missed the magic she'd found in evoking whole worlds entirely from words. She was, after all, a writer.

One day, after a long dry spell, a story occurred to her. The story concerned a journey she had taken with her children. It touched on all her most pressing obsessions.

Family *and* the world. Domestic *and* political. Not either/or. Both/and. Feverishly, she wrote up a proposal, thinking it through, checking it over, making sure it was the best that it could be. Then she printed it and left it on her desk for one last revision before sending it off to her agent. For the first time in many years, she felt excited and hopeful. This was her *real* material. She knew it.

209

That afternoon when she came home from work, her son—now on the verge of manhood—stood at her desk. His feet, a shoulder's width apart, seemed rooted to the floor. His face—that nose she'd wiped, those teeth she'd paid to straighten, those lips that had lisped his first words of love to her—was dark. He held the proposal in his hand. "Am I in this story?" he said.

The writer shivered, as at a sudden gust of wind. She watched the pages of her manuscript fly out of her son's hands and skirt the walls. Some of the pages sped out the window, scudded through the yard, and flapped against the trees and the telephone wires. Some of the pages soared up, up to the west, swooping and darting like seagulls until they disappeared in the wide dark. Some of those pages sped towards her open mouth, surged down her throat, gagged that scream that struggled to rise, wadded themselves into a lump, choked her.

"I don't want you to write about me," her son said.

The writer said nothing. There was nothing to say. She took the pages from her son and rent them to bits. Book Number Two did not appear.

Stop

Surgery to remove part or all of the larynx is a partial or total laryngectomy. In either operation, the surgeon performs a tracheostomy, creating an opening called a stoma in the front

of the neck.

A partial laryngectomy preserves the voice. After a brief recovery period the patient can breathe and talk in the usual way. In some cases, however, the voice may be hoarse or weak.

In a total laryngectomy, the whole voice box is removed, and the stoma is permanent. The patient breathes through the stoma and must learn to talk in a new way.

Fast Forward

I do not talk much to my classmates outside of workshop. But one day one of them spies me in the lunch line. "I've been thinking," she says. "People *do* write about their kids. They write about them all the time. Maybe we were a bit hasty in class."

This is generous of her; if anyone has reason to feel threatened by the essay I wrote, she does. She was once a foster child. Her story, while not identical to my daughter's, echoes those themes of loss and longing and violence.

She's right, of course. People do write about their kids. But often it seems they write print versions of those bare-bum-on-the-bear-rug photos. Gee willakers! What a little dickens! *Kids Say the Darnedest Things.* Their kids may hate them later, but more for lapses of taste than for any serious revelations about their lives.

Stop

"Voice in writing, identified variously as style, persona, stance, or ethos, has never been very clearly defined, and, as a consequence, there has never been a consistent methodology for how to use it in the teaching of writing. Although these definitional and methodological problems have frequently been chronicled in the journals (see, for example, Hashimoto; Leggo), the voice metaphor, which emerged in the 1970s, remains extraordinarily popular...and has a strong presence in contemporary discussions of writing."

Rewind

If you must write it, put it in a drawer.
Put it in a drawer? Who am I, Emily Dickinson?
Tell all the truth. But tell it slant.

Fast Forward

I meet on the grass with our Fellow. She of the pretty shoes, of the dire warnings and grave predictions. She who looks so beautiful and so serious and so exhausted on the jacket photo of her first book, a memoir about her heroin-addict mother.

I ask the question that's been bothering me. Was it something I said? Was there anything in that first essay—the one I brought to the class—was there anything in the *writing* that led her to believe I might treat this material in an exploitative way?

No, she says. It wasn't the writing. The writing was fine. But the situation is inherently exploitative. My daughter, I'd said, had been traumatized by her history of abandonment and orphanage neglect. To write a book about my daughter's trauma would be to re-inscribe it. It would be a huge betrayal. "To a non-writer, a book is the truth."

"Suppose I wrote a book of poems?"

"Oh." She pauses. "That would be okay. That would be different."

But why? Because nobody would read it?

Stop

Lana Turner was fifteen (according to her) or sixteen (according to most sources) on the day that Billy Wilkerson, a journalist with the *Hollywood Reporter*—a writer, not a talent scout—spotted her at the Top Hat Café, gave her his card, and told her to give him a call. Lana had no acting experience.

Rewind

I would worry about you if you pushed yourself into the limelight with this material. Bust foremost, like Lana Turner, the Sweater Girl. All flash, no substance.

Save yourself as a writer.

Save myself for what?

Having come to writing late (too afraid, too unsure, concerned that I didn't have a "voice"); having laboured already for nearly my full complement of the "ten years in the cold" once prophesied to apprentice writers by Ted Solotaroff; having published a long string of short pieces that may win awards but don't win me readers, I don't *want* to put aside my own ambitions. Not once I've found my material.

Renunciation is a part of the writing life.

I am no stranger to renunciation. I love my child without expectation of return. Must I love my work the same way?

Save yourself as a writer. It smacks of saving myself for 213 marriage. There is something illicit, even something erotic in the idea of telling truths about the people we love.

And everybody knows this: Mothers must renounce the erotic.

Fast Forward

Later, much later, I read my classmates' written comments. They do not sound like what got said in class. Sometimes that happens in workshops. A ball starts rolling and nobody can stop it. It picks up momentum and so much gets left behind. Now I can see that my classmates liked my writing. They thought I had an important story. They just didn't know if it could be, or should be, a book. They didn't know because they weren't experienced. None of them had written a book. (The instructors had written books, though, and they thought I should not write this one.)

Later still, I think about the people in that class. Most were daughters. Not one, if memory serves me, was the mother of a daughter. Not one.

Stop

Cheryl Crane was arrested and charged with the murder of Johnny Stompanato. Despite confusing evidence—including a lack of fingerprints on the weapon and an absence of blood at the scene—a coroner's inquest ruled it "justifiable homicide," and Cheryl went free. But she and Lana Turner remained estranged for a long time— according to some accounts, for almost forty years, until shortly before her mother's death.

Rewind

Writing this will irreparably ruin your relationship with your daughter.

I've often wondered whether I'm to blame. Whether that long separation for the first writers' conference was the cause or at least the catalyst for Maia's later anger and anxiety and violence. Her reactions at the time had seemed normal. She had welcomed me home. We'd slipped back into our routines like otters returning to water. The problems hadn't surfaced until later. They had seemed complex, so complex that the psychiatric labels couldn't cover them, so complex that no one cause could be found. But what if the reason had been staring us in the face? What if it was all my fault?

Your story reminds me of one that I want to write, about my friend, the priest who is also a pedophile.

I want to write about a child; my instructor wants to write about a pedophile. How can a child be like a pedophile?

You can't portray a pedophile as good in any way. You can't portray a child as bad in any way. People want the simple story.

Maybe the writer is the pedophile. Abuser. Exploiter.

Play

As Maia has matured, it's become clear that she has what teachers call an "auditory learning style." That is to say, she learns primarily by listening. She also shows a gift for words. Her puns startle and amuse. She reads aloud with enthusiasm and intonation, mimics newscasters and our guests, and can retell a story as told to her, exact in all its parts.

Fast Forward

It takes me almost a year to write this essay. To say that I am composing it would imply a calm deliberation I don't feel. Writing this is wrenching. But it's not like pulling teeth. Pulling teeth is a lot easier. At least you know what you are going after. This is more like pulling at entrails. Or untangling a knot. Looking for a thread that I can't find. And every time I do find it, every time I get a purchase, feel a loosening, something interrupts me. So I start. Stop. Start again. Go over what I've already done. Change it. Stop. Change it back.

Sometimes, I am the cause of these interruptions. Me. My own fears. My own worries. My own process and problems and angst. But often my daughter interrupts. She falls from a fence, needs stitches, and her hard-won calm shatters. So improved over the past months, she begins to rage and hit again, so each morning I sit at the computer with bruised forearms and a sense of discouragement. Then she gets the flu and I have to give up my writing hours to care for her. Then I am volunteering in her classroom; then it's her gym day and I need to pick her up early; the next day, she has an appointment with her therapist. That's what it's like.

Play

Listening to those tapes, I am struck by the energy in my voice. I'm no actor. But I read with expression and verve. Individuating each character, from Mortimer, who takes such glee in annoying everybody else, to Shy Charles, who doesn't like to talk. I'm the witch, the princess, the fairy godmother, and the wolf. I sound happy on those tapes. Even when impersonating a growling ogre. What I hear in those tapes is pure, uncomplicated, unconditional love. And that's what my daughter listened to, every night, from the time she was two until she was nearly six. The nights that I was gone and the nights that I was home. After her regular story-time, after her teeth were brushed and pajamas were on, after her snuggles and entreaties for just one more hug or a new glass of water, she'd press "play" and settle in for the nightly recording. During the day, I may have sounded—*must* have sounded—irritated, exhausted, sarcastic, judgemental, disappointed, even despairing at times. But at night, Maia heard different.

Stop

Stoma. Stompanato. Eerily similar sounds, the one an abbreviated other. Perhaps this irony occurred to Lana Turner as she lay, those last months, on her death bed. She was known for her sense of humour, so the thought might have tickled her. Tickled—then lodged in her throat, and become an irritation, an annoyance, maybe a sore. Unvoiced.

Play

Before my second trip to the conference, I made a new recording. Instead of a tape, I burned a CD, using the soundtrack on the movie software that came with my computer. It was rough, patched together, but passable, although the built-in mike kept cutting out on me and I had to rush through several of the stories. After recording forty minutes or so—poems I'd written for her, songs, a funny story about a boy who calls himself "King of the Blahs"—I realized that, this being a CD, there was lots of room for more. So I downloaded some Robert Munsch books from the web. Authors as popular as Munsch apparently can afford to give their work away. Maia loved the CD. But later she told me, "I wish it was just you on the CD. I like Robert Munsch and I like his stories. But I like your stories better. And I really like to listen to *your* voice."

Stop

"Literary critics often speak of 'presence' and 'codes' and 'intertextual discourse' when discussing voice, but writers can scarcely afford to be so theoretical or lofty in their approach. Voice is, to paraphrase Flannery O'Connor, the mud that we use to write."

Rewind

Mama's *voices*. Charming mistake, or startling insight? Even on a cheap kids' tape recorder, you can always hear more than one.

Record

Like any curious child, Maia liked to play with the buttons on her tape recorder and to experiment with the amplifying feature on its microphone. Parts of those old tapes are blank now, where she has erased them. Parts of them sound with her own words. In her own voice.

Answering Moneta

The year I turned fifteen, I rose at five on Saturday mornings. It took me half an hour to fix my hair. I was wearing it Dutch-boy style with the ends turned under all around, and I had to crimp it twice with the curling iron to prevent it from separating into ragged, uneven clumps. The bangs were the trickiest part. I could not get close to them without grazing the wand against my already scarred and pimple-blotted forehead. Outside, the rising sun stained the pine trees in silhouette. Robins and blackbirds sang. Inside, the stench of scorched hair summoned tears; tears fogged my glasses; my glasses slid down my flat-bridged, oily nose. I would never get it right. Yanking the plug from the wall, I squinted at my watch. Only fifteen minutes to catch the bus. I pulled on jeans, a T-shirt, last year's buffalo sandals, then stuffed the uniform—crisp, with pink and white vertical stripes—into a plastic bag. I never put it on at home. I always waited until I got inside the hospital.

In the summer of 1810, John Keats left school and was apprenticed to an apothecary-surgeon named Thomas

Hammond. He appears to have gone willingly, even eagerly, his decision possibly influenced by the fact that Hammond was the attending doctor throughout the recent fatal illness of his mother. Frances Keats suffered from tuberculosis, the disease that already had killed her brother and would eventually take each of her three sons. John, the eldest and most possessively devoted, appointed himself her nurse and primary caregiver. During his school breaks, he would stay awake all night in the chair beside her bed. He prepared her food, administered her medicines, and read novels aloud to her by the hour. She died in March.

220

A few months later, as Hammond's new apprentice, he must have undertaken similar duties—sweeping and stocking the surgery, taking notes on cases, and helping with standard interventions such as leeching, cupping, blistering, and poulticing. In October, he turned fifteen.

My first day at the hospital, the nurse on duty eyed me doubtfully from behind thick-lensed spectacles. "A candy-striper? Nobody bothered to tell *us*." She heaved herself to her feet. "I suppose we'll find something for you to do."

In the beginning, I liked the work. I did the jobs the nurses or orderlies were too busy for. I straightened sheets and made beds. I pushed a library cart from room to room. I delivered flowers and cards, brought cool water and ginger ale, and took away dirty dishes.

I also listened to the patients.

This was the real job, I came to understand. This was what they needed. The old ones, especially. Even here,

in their double and triple rooms, where "privacy" meant
a thin cotton curtain between the beds, they had nobody
to talk to.

The nurses warned me not to get too chummy. "Its
fine to chat with them, dear, but don't let anybody
monopolize you. And if they offer you a tip or a gift,
under *no circumstances* may you take it."

Mrs. Franklin hadn't heard this rule. She was in her
eighties, brittle and bent with osteoporosis, but determined to keep up appearances. She could not bear the
pale blue hospital gowns, and she refused to wear a house-
coat in the daytime. Instead, with stiff, deliberate fingers,
she fastened each tiny mother-of-pearl button on the
cotton print dresses and wool cardigans she'd brought
from home. She had come to have her cataracts taken
care of; while in the hospital she had developed pneumo-
nia, and because she lived alone, her doctors had decided
to keep her there for a few weeks, until the danger passed.
The cataract operation had not been a complete success;
her vision in the future would be compromised. Reading
would be difficult. Driving, impossible.

She was a talker. In my brief trips through her room I
learned about her family—two boys, one a lawyer. About
her late husband, who had managed a local bank. About
her church and its new minister. About her garden.
Whenever she heard the squeak of the library cart, she
would beckon me to bring it closer; although the print
on the books was too fine now for her eyes, she got pleasure just from sniffing their spines. She liked to tell me
about her favourites and to quiz me about my own. It
became a routine for us. Later, when I had finished my

shift for the day, sometimes I would linger by her doorway, waiting to wish her goodbye.

Early in July she was discharged. I found her seated in the chair, black shoes neatly laced and her suitcase packed and waiting on the floor. "My son's coming," she said. "He'll be here shortly." She fumbled with the clasp on her handbag. "Here. I want you to have this."

It was a gold Cross pen, an elegant, fine-tipped ballpoint. Her initials were engraved on its clip.

"Mrs. Franklin...I can't. Thank you, but no."

"Yes." Out in the hall an elevator door opened, and a man's firm footsteps sounded across the tiles.

"Please. I'm not allowed."

"Who's going to know?" She pulled me closer and dropped the pen into the deep, striped pocket of my uniform. "There." Her smile was like the Cheshire cat's. "Now, help me up, dear. I believe my son has arrived."

Throughout his five-year apprenticeship, Keats spent free afternoons with his old friend and teacher, Charles Cowden Clarke. Day after day he tramped the two miles of fields and footpaths between Edmonton, where Hammond had his surgery, and Enfield, his old school. Day after day the two young men talked politics and read poetry. Cowden Clarke introduced Keats to Tasso and Milton and Spenser. Keats responded, "ramping" through *The Faerie Queene* like a "young horse turned into a spring meadow." Shortly afterwards, he began to write poetry himself.

Meanwhile, his duties at the surgery became progressively more demanding. Within his first year he began formal studies in physiology, anatomy, and *materia medica*—what we would call pharmacology today. He also attended post mortems and helped with the delivery of babies. Under Hammond's supervision he learned how to mix medicines, dress wounds, pull teeth, and lance abscesses. Some contemporaries argued that these tasks might jeopardize the health or sanity of a boy under the age of sixteen, and Keats did at times become depressed. But if his dark moods persuaded him that he would be better off pursuing another line of work, no evidence survives to prove it. In 1815, when his apprenticeship ended, far from running away from a medical career, he registered for a full year of lectures at Guy's Hospital in London. His decision to enroll for a full year rather than the six months required of apothecaries suggests that initially, at least, he was aiming for the more prestigious and demanding surgeon's licentiate. Despite the time and energy he was devoting to poetry, he appears to have been a conscientious, dedicated, and even gifted student.

223

Early in his term at Guy's he was appointed dresser to the surgeon William Lucas. This was a coveted position involving extra responsibilities as well as opportunities for closer observation of surgical procedures. Yet Lucas was renowned for his clumsiness. Continual exposure to botched operations may have contributed to Keats's decision in July 1816 to sit the Society of Apothecaries' examination instead. By this time he had acquired a reputation among his classmates as a man of fancy, lost in daydreams instead of focused on the study of anatomy. Several of them predicted he would fail. When their pre-

dictions were disappointed—Keats passed, *they* failed—
they could not disguise their jealousy. It's only because
he's good at Latin, one said. The exam wasn't a test of
real medical skill. This was not an opinion shared by
Astley Cooper, senior surgeon at Guy's, who believed
that standards on the examinations were high. In truth,
Keats had graduated from a challenging program at the
youngest possible age, in the shortest possible time. By
any measure, his success was a significant achievement.

One day I arrived at the hospital to discover that my job
had changed. No more patient contact.

Why? If anyone ever told me, I've forgotten.
Although the golden pen was still a cool weight in my
uniform pocket, I am sure nobody had discovered it.
Maybe the Ladies' Auxiliary—older volunteers—were
pulling rank. Maybe they, or the nurses or orderlies, had
decided that some jobs were too delicate, too important
to be left to a mere child. Maybe another candy striper
had broken down at some glimpse of suffering. *Was* there
another candy striper? I wasn't aware of any. This was
the seventies, era of the "Me generation," and volunteering was not popular among my peers.

The nurse's crepe-soled shoes squeaked as she strode,
three steps ahead of me, across the gleaming tiles. My
task for the remainder of the summer was to clean a
storage closet. Gesturing to the cluttered cupboards, she
told me to wash beakers and fold linens, to line disinfec-
tant liquids up on one shelf and sterile containers along
another.

"Okay," I said.

The first day wasn't too bad. I hummed while I sorted and scrubbed.

The next week there was less to do. The time dragged. My fingers drifted to my pocket and fretted with the pen. I knew the breeze outside was warm. My friends would only now be waking. In an hour or two they would congregate at somebody's pool or under a willow near the lake and snap open Cokes or light clandestine cigarettes. The scent of coconut lotion would glut the air.

It's not as if I'm getting paid, I thought.

I lasted a couple more weeks. Then one morning when the bus pulled into the downtown station, instead of waiting as I usually did for it to resume its hospital route, I pushed open the back door and stumbled onto the sidewalk. I didn't know what I intended; I had no intentions at all. Aimlessly, listlessly, I wandered—past shuttered stores and houses, past the silent library—until at last, in the oldest part of town, I came to a street that terminated in a tiny park. Not much more than a scrap of sand, with an overhanging maple and the sound of the lake licking the rocks. I sat looking east toward the city, whose towers always loomed in my inner geography. Yellow maple keys fluttered onto my head and shoulders. Gulls flapped and screeched offshore. After a while I fished for the gold pen, groped for the school scribbler I'd stuffed in my bag before leaving home. Under the sharp sun its pages were too bright, too blank. In a kind of dizzy dream I closed my eyes against the glare, then opened them. And wrote.

In an 1818 letter to John Taylor, his publisher and friend, Keats argued that poetry "...should strike the Reader as a wording of his own highest thoughts, and appear almost a Remembrance." That is how his fragment "The Fall of Hyperion" struck me. Reading it first as an adult, I did not come to it, as most of us come to his more famous odes, with layers of half-conscious association filtering my view. Instead, I came to it chaste, without expectation or desire—without even, I confess, much interest—for who, these days, gets excited about "Miltonic verse"? Keats himself, in explaining his decision to abandon the piece, implied that its inversions and elevated diction were hopelessly old-fashioned and irrelevant.

Yet, for all my resistance to the poem, it spoke to me, spoke "out loud and bold," in a key I recognized as my own. Settling with my book into the wing chair in the corner of my study, pushing aside the stack of unmarked student assignments waiting there, I placed a steaming cup of tea on a nearby table. The room was still and silent as I read—the big, claret-coloured anthology resting on my knee, as weighty and dense as a bible. In the margins of its onion-skin pages my felt-tipped pen left palimpsests wherever I had written before. The room was still and silent; I read on. Only the whisper of those pages as I turned them disturbed the calm. Only the whisper of those pages and the urgency of the poet's voice.

The first canto of "The Fall of Hyperion" takes the form of a dream vision. The speaker describes a beautiful and fertile place, where the refuse of a feast is spread. Hunger grows in him, "more yearning" than any he has felt on earth, and because the food is plentiful, he eats and drinks. The juice he swallows turns out to be a potion that puts him to sleep; when he wakes, he is in the presence of an altar. Approaching it gingerly, he hears the voice of Moneta, goddess of memory and warning, who commands him to ascend the stairs or die. Conscious of the "tyranny" of Moneta's demand and awed by the "hard task proposed," he soon *feels* her "fierce threat" as his body takes on the cold weight and numbness of death. At the last possible second he forces his foot onto the second stair. Vitality returns, and he races to the top. Once there, he enters into conversation with the goddess. Why was he saved, he wants to know.

> "...Thou hast felt
> What 'tis to die and live again before
> Thy fated hour, that thou hadst power to do so
> Is thy own safety..."

None is permitted to ascend the steps, she replies, save "those to whom the miseries of the world / Are misery, and will not let them rest." Imagination is the poet's protection—imagination, and empathy for others. For Moneta is the last of the Titans, a vanished race of gods, and she holds within her mind the secrets of the past. But although she offers to share this knowledge, until the speaker stops brooding about his own suffering and acknowledges hers, the scenes of desolation swirling through her brain remain invisible to him. To create art worthy of the name, Keats seems to say, we must actively strive to see and understand.

This paraphrase does not begin to do justice to the poem's complexity or its power, which lies less in the story it tells than in the voice that tells the story. That voice is a distinctive amalgam of poetic assurance and doubt, a peculiarly modern, self-conscious voice—one that uses art to ask questions about art's uses. The initial verse prelude provides a frame of reference for the succeeding narrative and emphasizes the uncertainties lurking beneath its surface. There, Keats distinguishes the "dumb enchantment" and escapism of fanatics' dreams from the articulate dream of poetry, while admitting some confusion about which kind of dream this one is. In his conversation with Moneta he begs her to reassure him that the poet is a "sage; / A humanist, physician to all men," and she apparently concedes, replying:

> "...The poet and the dreamer are distinct,
> Diverse, sheer opposite, antipodes.
> The one pours out a balm upon the World,
> The other vexes it."

Yet only a moment before, she was denigrating him as a "dreaming thing," and challenging him to justify his existence: "What benefit canst thou, or all thy tribe / To the great world? ...think of the Earth." While he angrily distinguishes himself from all "mock lyrists, large self worshipers / And careless Hectorers in proud bad verse," his doubt about his identity remains. Is his a "fire spell of words" fit to soothe an ailing humanity, or merely the self-indulgent babble of a narcissistic fool? This tension is never resolved. Long after I closed the book, his poignant question lingered: "What am I then: Thou spakest of my tribe: / What tribe?"

Make a contribution.
Those words—my father's. Already at age fifteen they were inscribed upon my brain. Nobody told me to sign up for candystriping. Nobody had to. *Make a contribution.* Week after week I tried to banish the refrain as, instead of going, as I should have, to the hospital, I wandered to the lake and wrote. My parents did not know. My friends did not know. For all I knew, even the nurses did not know that I wasn't still crouched in that closet, perpetually cleaning. But I knew. I knew I was sloughing off—giving up, giving in, doing my own thing, failing to do the right thing—in the worst, the most cravenly escapist way.

Make a contribution.
Why did I never consider a career in medicine? When I was very young, people would sometimes ask me if I intended to become a nurse, like my father. "My dad's a doctor," I'd sullenly reply, conscious already of the difference in status between the two roles, insulted they'd assign me the lesser one. Candystriping only exacerbated this resentment. What I saw in the hospital was hierarchy: men bossing women, older women bossing younger

women, healthy people bossing sick people. Having excelled at science in my first few years of high school, I purposely failed out of chemistry. Dropped math. Neglected to sign up for physics. I want to be a writer, I said. I don't need to know that stuff.

Make a contribution.
Words on that sun-splashed beach leapt and sprang from my golden pen, spilled onto page after page. I carried them like treasures through the days. But I could not rid my mind of my father's admonition, and so from its earliest beginnings, writing for me was laced as certainly to guilt as it was to discovery and pleasure.

Until his mother's death, Keats was an indifferent student, but in his grief he turned to books for solace and escape. Once he began to write, that proved an even greater comfort. A childhood neighbour of the Keatses later remembered that as a small boy, John, instead of replying seriously to questions put to him, would make up rhymes to the last words spoken and then laugh. That delight in language never left him. His letters to his friends—so often deeply reflective—are swiftly digressive, too, and overflowing with puns, bits of bawdy, and music, meter, rhyme. Love like that is a mystery—as much a part of us as the rhythm of our breath or the whorl of our fingerprints. Love like that can't be denied, and Keats did not bother to try. When he told his guardian, Richard Abbey, that he didn't intend to work

as an apothecary after all, but meant to try his hand at
poetry, Abbey called him a "Silly Boy," and "prophesied
a speedy Termination to his inconsiderate Enterprise."
But Keats knew his abilities were "greater than most"
men's. He recognized vocation when he felt it. At the   231
same time, he never gave away his medical books and
with friends often deliberated about returning to practise. "I am ambitious of doing the world some good," he
said. "If I should be spared, that may be the work of
maturer years—in the interval I will assay to reach as
high a summit in Poetry as the nerve bestowed upon me
will suffer." In theory, he thought "fine doing" most
important, but in practise he gave priority to the writing.

Make a contribution.
Say it out loud. It is a trochaic line. A strong beat followed by a weak beat, a kind of falling motion. While
the iamb, in which a weak stress precedes a strong one,
is the most frequently used meter in English verse, and
few poems are composed entirely in trochaic meter,
trochaic inversion is not uncommon, particularly at the
beginning or in the middle of lines. Where trochees
remain unusual—even rare—is at the end of a line—in
the terminal position. And the terminal trochee's
acknowledged master, according to Paul Fussell, is Keats.
He uses the trochee "as if to establish…a tone of…intel-
ligent ingenuousness," and to reinforce a mood of "sim-
plicity" and "sincerity." That note of sincerity sounded
also in my father's voice:

Make a contribution.

Although in skilful hands the terminal trochee can be used to convey an earnest appeal, in the poetry of our own century it more often has expressed exhausted derision and irony. For, as Fussell explains, where the overall context is skeptical, a descending line's effect is sardonic.

Make a contribution.

The overall context *is* skeptical.

Keats called the English Regency a "barbarous" age. War raged almost constantly, unemployment and poverty went unchecked, and radical political dissent was met with outright violence. Personal life was no less painful. As he knew better than anyone, even a "middle class" childhood could be scarred by the early assumption of adult responsibilities and early exposure to adult suffering. By the age of fourteen the poet had lost his father, his mother, his grandfather, an uncle, and a brother. By the age of twenty-three he had lost his two remaining brothers—one to emigration, one to tuberculosis. By twenty-four he had fallen in love and fallen out of health. He died at twenty-five.

Our own age poses a different risk. Rather than requiring us to grow up too fast, it defies us to grow up at all. Barring extreme poverty and illness—rarer now, at least in the developed world, than they were in the 19th century—the escapist dream-state of adolescence can achieve an indefinite extension. Responsibility can be delayed; loss can be denied. But has this prolonged youth of ours made the world a better place? If in Keats's day it

remained barely possible amid the chaos to cling to the
ideal of a palliative art, in our own day this ideal seems,
on the face of it, preposterous. Our privileged lives may
be comfortable and secure, but much of the world is still
miserable. The gaps between rich and poor, strong and
weak, healthy and ill have not diminished. Meanwhile,
prosperity gives rise to technology, and technology, wed
to complacency, spawns evils so vast, so extreme, that
they can scarcely be imagined. Will art soothe the pain
of Auschwitz, Hiroshima, Cambodia, Rwanda, Kosovo,
Iraq? Can art even heal my Mrs. Franklin, with her eyes,
like Moneta's, so "planetary," so sightless? Keats condemned his own age. What might he have said about
ours? If he lived today, what would he sing about in "full-
throated ease" from beneath the fragrant plum tree in
the pleasant Hampstead garden?

During the early decades of the 19th century, physicians
generally profited from an improvement in their profes-
sion's reputation, but the contributions of my father's
specialty, pathology, remained unrecognised. Though
the microscope existed, the great advances in cellular
pathology and microbiology—including the isolation of
the tubercle bacillus and the discovery of antibiotics that
might have saved John Keats's life—still belonged to the
future. Because people persisted in the belief that the
dead would rise on Judgement Day, even autopsy was
rarely performed. Dismemberment was thought to deny
the dead person both a proper funeral and a decent
burial. Progressive thinkers such as Keats's teacher,

Astley Cooper, fully understood the importance of hands-on learning for the advancement of medical knowledge. ("Nothing ever becomes real till it is experienced," Keats would later argue, echoing his lessons at Guy's.) But the value of experience was less obvious to the public, and so the use of bodies for anatomy classes remained forbidden by law. In response to this situation, the practise of "body-snatching" flourished. The body-snatchers, or "resurrection men," as they were also called, would rob local graves by night, bring the naked corpses, in sacks, to the hospital's dissecting room before dawn, and collect their fee from Cooper, who also paid their fines and supported their families if they were caught. Beneficial to medical science as the custom undoubtedly was, the horror surrounding it is, perhaps, understandable. From the perspective of the ordinary person, anatomists or pathologists exposed too much; they had altogether too close a contact with the mystery.

Writers are sometimes accused of similar trespasses. Personal or "confessional" writers, who tell about ourselves, violate the taboo against showing. We must not put ourselves at the centre, for that is solipsistic, narcissistic, limited, self-indulgent. And writers who focus on the lives of others are no less feared or deplored. To write about another person—especially without the drapery and disguise of fiction—is inevitably, like the anatomist, to use a human being in the service of a truth. To write about almost anything, it seems, is to trespass against decorum and "decent burial."

The horror surrounding the practise is, perhaps, understandable.

The "Fall of Hyperion" can be read as a kind of parable about the writing life. Awe at the wealth of the inherited tradition gives way to a hunger to contribute to it. Sensual pleasure in "the refuse" of that feast, and intoxication with one's own developing powers, mark a writer's initiation. But these heady beginnings lead inevitably, if one continues, to deepened insight and a paralyzing awareness, not only of human suffering, but of one's own meager capacity to illuminate—or alleviate— the pains of our existence.

Keats's first, tentative poems were deeply personal— elegies for beloved people, tributes to beloved writers, and celebrations of his friendships, written in the intimate and relatively relaxed form of "epistles." Later poems catalogued his fantasies of love. The critics mocked these early efforts, accusing him of self-indulgence and "effeminacy." Although the bad reviews did not *kill* him, as Shelley and Byron later maintained, they surely must have stung him, and made him conscious, in new ways, of his audience. So he must have anticipated that by writing so nakedly in "The Fall" about the use and value of poetry, he risked the same charges of solipsism and narcissism that he levelled there against other poets. For him, this was no trivial matter. Like all the Romantics, he nurtured grand aims for his work. Poetry, he believed, was a serious calling, every bit as important as his earlier commitment to medicine. Having initially sought—and found—escape and pleasure in both reading and writing, he wanted now to believe they could mean more. If medicine could heal the body, poetry, he hoped, could heal the soul. Yet, as "The Fall"

itself suggests, neither his character nor his poetic practise allowed him to rest easy in that belief.

In his biography of the poet, Andrew Motion details a
walk Keats once took on Hampstead Heath with
Cowden Clarke. Ambling along in their usual way,
talking of poetry and mutual friends, they were startled
by the sudden appearance of an angry bull, escaped from
its tether. Just when the animal seemed about to attack
them, they managed to calm it by staring straight into its
eyes.

Staring straight at the subject—the steady, unflinch-
ing gaze. In his life, as in his work, Keats strove incessantly to master this. Calling for a candle on the night in
February, 1820 when he first coughed blood, he stood for
a moment examining the spot. His housemate, Charles
Armitage Brown, reported: "After regarding it stead-
fastly, he looked up in my face, with a calmness of countenance that I can never forget, and said, 'I know the
colour of that blood;—it is arterial blood;—I cannot be
deceived in that colour;—that drop of blood is my death
warrant;—I must die.'" Later, in Italy, when his year of
"posthumous existence" finally drew to a close, he still
refused to pretend or deny. "Have you ever seen anyone
die?" he said to Severn, his terrified friend and resident
candystriper. No? "Well, then. I pity you…what trouble
and danger you have got into for me."

He was speaking from experience. Just over two years
earlier he had sat deathbed attendance on his beloved
brother Tom. Sometimes the sorrow and the pressure
grew too heavy for him, and he had to leave the room

and immerse himself in his work, in poetry, to get away from the sight of Tom's already ghostly face and the sound of his plaintive voice. Who could blame him? Given the pains and difficulties of his existence, it is no wonder that Keats sometimes used writing as an escape. Besides, an escape like his, into serious application, scarcely deserves the name. The exercise of imagination may have been therapeutic to him, but he never allowed his delight in it to blind him to the "miseries of the world" or the requirements of his art.

237

Although "The Fall of Hyperion" is in part an attack on the use of poetic imagination for escape, the poem itself takes the form of a dream vision. This may not be the paradox it seems. The uses of imagination are one thing, Keats seems to say—but its sources are another. We take our inspiration where we find it. Dreams are no more suspect in this context than the daily news or the works of our literary forebears. Even memory, even our own self-doubt may serve as muse—whatever moves us to wonder or anger or awe, whatever moves us to speculation. Art should end in empathy and compassion for the world, but it begins with desire. With hunger.

I kept the gold pen for many years. In college I was still carrying it, stuffed randomly amid the jumble of a large and heavy shoulder bag. By now its engraving had faded and its surface was nicked and scratched. I used it for a journal—the only form of writing, aside from academic papers, that I managed to keep up with during that confusing and lonely period of my life. No doubt my book was full of brooding reflections and pained descriptions of my hopeless, helpless feelings, as most adolescent journals are. Whatever else it held I don't know, because I didn't save it. In my second year I dated someone who learned of its existence. "Talk about self-indulgent," he said. "How can you do that? Don't you feel silly? That kind of writing is so narcissistic." In the spell of silence that followed this pronouncement the golden pen disappeared. I didn't think of it again until I started working on this book.

The Story Lab

Picture a man. You'll find him in the lab. He has a face like Johnny Carson's—the same lift to the eyebrows, the same cheeky humour—but there's darkness, too in the shrewd eyes and the determined set of his mouth, and compassion in the *Drive carefully* that he calls to his technicians as, one by one, they finish work and head for home. What kind of doctor specializes in pathology? One whose hands are too shaky for the surgery, he sometimes jokes. Or maybe one whose heart is too tender to let him be the bearer of bad news.

It's getting late. Time to stop. He rises reluctantly from his microscope, labels one last vial, double-checks the settings on the cryostat. "See you tomorrow," he calls to the techs on night duty. Then he unclips his dictaphone, slips the noose of the stethoscope, and shrugs off his white coat. The leather soles of his loafers tap-tap against the polished floors.

In the parking lot, trees cast long shadows. He slides onto the seat of his blue Oldsmobile and drives. To his right glints a lake. All along the roadside, the gardens of the grand waterfront houses bloom. Out of the corner of his eye he takes these in, trying to ward off worse sights, sights that rise in his mind's eye all unbidden. Sights like the bodies of the teenagers he autopsied last week— mangled and burnt beyond recognition following their post-prom crash. Sights like the bloated boater who went out without his life jacket, or the woman, his mother's age, riddled with a cancer she wasn't aware she had. Sights like the dark smudges under the eyes of the child whose leukemia he confirmed that morning. Try as he might, he can't banish these images com- pletely; they cling like the smell of formaldehyde to his skin, haunting him whether he's sleeping or awake.

At home, he showers, swallows a quick meal and heads to his garage for the manual mower. He's tired. The lawn is large and wide, with a deep ditch. It takes forty minutes of steady work to cut the grass, forty minutes of pushing and pulling. He doesn't feel like doing this job. But the grass is long and tomorrow's fore- cast calls for rain. In the pauses between rows, when the shrill scissor blades fall silent, he hears the voices of his daughter and the neighbourhood kids calling out to each other in a game of hide-and-seek. *Allee allee in free.*

By now, it's twilight. From the front step he watches the robins resume the meal he interrupted with his work. The kids, who've finished their game, race across the street and clamber up the lawn's incline to where he sits. Heedless of bruises or bumps, they tease and jostle and push and finally throw themselves at his feet. "It's late," he tells them. "Time to go in for bed." "Sure," they agree. "But only if you tell us a story."

And so he does. The bright faces in front of him are so eager and insistent. He would like to please them. But how can he begin? It isn't easy for him; stories do not, as a rule, come tripping from this man's tongue. He likes to deal in facts. In what is known. He's not much for making things up. And he can hardly tell them about his day; the sights and sounds of the morgue are not for children. The only benign thing on his mind right now is the weather. The weather, and maybe their own names, simple and sweet and short as the grass he's just trimmed.

So that's where he starts. With Robbie, a boy who used to hide his face behind his mother's skirts, and who, at eight, can still give way easily to tears, He calls him Robbie Raindrop. Then Sandra. "Sand," the other kids call her, which makes him think of the beach, and sun, and so he names her Sandra Sunshine. Then there is Suzanne, who seems spoiled and insistent and temperamental; he'll call her Suzanne Sleet. And finally, his own Suzie, born in a blizzard—she's Suzie Snowflake, of course. The other boy's name, Doug, poses a challenge. He can't think of a kind of weather beginning with the letter D. "Doug," he muses. "Doug." This kid seems a little lost, somehow—uncentred, like the snack the man grabbed at the hospital cafeteria that morning. "Dougie Doughnut," he says, testing the idea. "Dougie Doughnut?" the kids echo, skeptically. "Yeah. Dougie Doughnut," he answers, more certain this time.

The story he tells them is episodic and picaresque. For its settings, he looks around him, at the apple trees and the lake a few blocks distant, at the storm sewers with their muskrats, at the gardens with their hidden toads. For its plot, he looks to familiar events. Even in this quiet suburb, adventure abounds. One night, near-hurricane winds knocked the roof from a house still under construction. Another time, a visiting cousin swallowed poison; he knows because he took the call. And once, a neighbour strung fishing line across the street to interrupt the progress of some motorcyclists. They'd blasted through that barrier, so the next night he threw paint at their heads when they refused to stop.

All these stories sound different to the children when they become the heroes, embroidered with their newly made names. They shriek and laugh and beg him to keep talking. So for the next few weeks of the long summer evenings, this becomes their routine. Each night they sit at his feet and beg him to talk; each night he delivers a new instalment.

Eventually, of course, he runs out of ideas. Or maybe he just gets bored. He tries to switch to a different kind of tale, something well-worn and familiar, something he's heard before and won't have to link to their own lives, something altogether made up, and made up long ago by someone else. Something that will prevent the need for thinking. But the kids won't have it. "No!" they exclaim. "No!" Their eyes glisten. Their voices ring in the night air. "Don't tell us that kind of story," they insist. "We don't want a fairy story. Tell us a story about ourselves."

Notes on the Essays

This is a book of non-fiction. The stories I tell are supported by research and observation but they are largely based on memory. Memory, of course, is notoriously fallible and partial, and some of the people depicted here as characters might see events quite differently than I do. In fact, as I hope the essays themselves make clear, I see things differently myself, depending on the lens I bring to bear on the material. In the memoir and personal essay, as in the art of pathological diagnosis, perspective is everything.

I have changed most names and identifying details to protect people's privacy. Fictional passages appear in several of the essays and will, I trust, be identifiable from their context.

All dictionary definitions, unless otherwise noted, are drawn from the *Oxford English Dictionary*.

"Pathology"

Page 2: The quotation comes from *An Introduction to General Pathology, 3rd Edition*, by the late W.G. Spector, revised by T.D. Spector (Edinburgh: Churchill Livingstone, 1989) 1.

Quotations that follow throughout the essay, apart from dictionary definitions, are from the same source. Used with the gracious permission of Dr. T. D. Spector. The definition of "inflammation" on page 14 is paraphrased.

"The Other Country"

Page 23: For the idea that disease and illness are distinguishable, I'm grateful to Jacalyn Duffin, *History of Medicine: A Scandalously Short Introduction* (Toronto: University of Toronto Press, 2000) 66-68. Thanks also to Dr. Duffin for welcoming me, a non-medical student, to her always engaging lectures at Queen's University.

Page 23: Heart and Stroke Foundation, "Get Your Blood Pressure Under Control." www.heartandstroke.ca.

Page 25: Oliver Sacks, *An Anthropologist on Mars* (New York: Alfred A. Knopf, 1995) Preface.

Page 26: Virginia Woolf, *On Being Ill* (Ashfield, MA: Paris Press, 2002) 11-12. Used by permission of The Society of Authors as the Literary Representative of the Estate of Virginia Woolf.

"On Separation"

Definitions in this essay come from WordNet: http://wordnet.princeton.edu/.

Page 39: www.eggology.com.

"Such Good Girls"

Page 75: "BPD [bi-polar disorder] is diagnosed predominantly (about 75%) in females." Andrew E. Skodol and Donna S.

Bender, "Why Are Women Diagnosed Borderline More Than Men?" *Psychiatric Quarterly*, 74 4 (December, 2003) 349-360.

"How To Be a Volunteer"

Page 93: Richard Marius, *A Writer's Companion*, 4th Edition (Boston: McGraw-Hill College, 1999).

Page 97: E.M. Forster, *Aspects of the Novel* (Harmondsworth, Middlesex: Penguin, 1976).

Page 103: Michael Holroyd, "Smoke with Fire: On The Ethics of Biography," *Works on Paper: The Craft of Biography and Autobiography* (Washington: Counterpoint, 2002) 19.

Page 103: E.M. Forster, *Howard's End* (New York Norton, 1998) Chapter 22.

"Female Troubles"

Page 115: Infertility statistics: http://www.asrm.org/Patients/faqs.html.

Page 116: Mark Perloe M.D. and Linda Gail Christie, *Miracle Babies Online and other Happy Endings*. Http://www.ivf.com/tocmb.html.

Page 120: Dr. Aniruddha Malpani, M.D. and Dr. Anjali Malpani, M.D. *How to Have a Baby: Overcoming Infertility*. Chapter 37: Myths and Misconceptions. http://www.infertilitybooks.com/onlinebooks/malpani/chapter37.html.

"At Lingyin Si"

Orphanage statistics: Laura Cecere, *The Children Can't Wait: China's Emerging Model for Intercountry Adoption* (Cambridge, MA: China Seas, 1998) 17.

Orphanage populations seemed to swell in the late 1980s through the 1990s, to the point where some institutions did not have enough beds for all the children coming to their doors. Some expanded to meet demand; in poorer institutions, children slept two or three to a crib. Recently, fewer children appear to be abandoned, or at least this is the official reason given by the China Center for Adoption Affairs for the decrease in "available children" for international adoption and their decision to tighten requirements for prospective international adopters.

The decrease in abandonments is attributed to a number of factors: increased prosperity (meaning families simply pay the fine for over-quota children); changes to local Family Planning strictures; government propaganda and policies designed to persuade rural families to keep their female children; selective abortion. http://research-china.blogspot.com/2006/06/hague-agreement-and-chinas.html.

Contrary to what some Westerners believe, domestic adoption also occurs in China. Traditionally, arrangements were informal and, for a variety of reasons, many prospective adoptive parents continue to prefer an informal process. Even so, more children in the orphanages are placed domestically than internationally; most orphanages are not part of the international program and of those that are, the ratio of domestic to international adoptions appears to range from about 5:1 to 3:1. The new regulations have made it somewhat easier to arrange a formal domestic adoption, so increased domestic adoption may also account for a small reduction in the number of children available for international adoption.

However, see also Brian Stuy, who argues that the orphanages still prefer to arrange international adoptions where possible, either for the funds these generate or because orphanage directors sincerely believe that internationally adopted children will enjoy a better quality of life than those who are domestically adopted. http://research-china.blogspot.com/2006/01/domestic-adoption-in-chinas-orphanages.html. Kay

Ann Johnson (see below) generally agrees with Stuy; both argue that in continuing to place relatively high numbers of children internationally, China is in contravention of the Hague Convention on Children's Rights, to which it is a signatory.

Whether or not abandonment is decreasing, all observers agree that many children—particularly disabled children—still find their way to orphanage doors, and if they remain there, their future prospects are poor, since they are unregistered, meaning that they do not qualify for most education and employment opportunities or other basic rights.

Orphanage conditions: Human Rights Watch, *Death by Default: A Policy of Fatal Neglect in China's State Orphanages* (January, 1996). www.hrw.org/summaries/s.china961.html. Human Rights Watch argues that there is a state *policy* of extermination and intentional abuse of abandoned infants in China. However, see also Kay Ann Johnson, *Wanting a Daughter, Needing a Son: Abandonment, Adoption and Orphanage Care in China* (St. Paul, Minnesota: Yeong and Yeong, 2004), as well as Johnson's earlier work in *Population and Development Review* for a somewhat different perspective. Johnson argues that while mortality is indeed high in many institutions, this is because many of the children arrive at the understaffed, underfunded orphanages already in extremely poor health, premature, or with congenital disabilities—and that in most cases, orphanage staff do their best under difficult circumstances to secure appropriate medical care. Anecdotal reports from adoptive parents suggest that their children's health when adopted varies widely. The most mildly affected suffer from skin and respiratory infections and developmental delays; some are malnourished, more severely delayed, or scarred from abuse. Add to that the more subtle, complex, and long-term physiological and emotional effects of abandonment and institutionalization, along with prenatal malnutrition, exposure to toxic chemicals, and high levels of stress hormones.

Page 127: Quotations of Marco Polo's writings here and following are taken from Manuel Komroff, rev. ed., *The Travels of Marco Polo [The Venetian]* (New York: Liveright, 1982). Used by permission.

248

For background on Lingyin Si and Hangzhou, I consulted David Leffman, Simon Lewis and Jermy Atiyah, *China: The Rough Guide* (London: Rough Guides Ltd., 2000) 437, 444.

Page 127: Hangzhou economy: http://www.hzindus.gov.cn/en/investment.asp#.

Page 129: Most researchers agree that abandoning families are prosecuted only about 25 per cent of the time; however, this rate varies considerably by region, and many families fear the penalties. Johnson, 91-92.

Page 131: Hangzhou income: http://www.hzindus.gov.cn/en/list.asp?id=732. Income in this wealthy region has risen since 2000; however, potential fines for abandonment in proportion to income remain extremely high.

Page 135: Inventions: http://library.thinkquest.org/15618/inventor.htm.

Page 135: Current population: World Health Organization, www.wpro.who.int/countries/chn/, among other sources.

Page 135: Problems with census, rural families ignoring one-child rule: Elizabeth Rosenthal, "Rural Flouting of One-Child Policy Undercuts China's Census," *New York Times*, April 14, 2000.

Page 135: Migrant worker population: http://communicatinglabourrights.wordpress.com/2008/02/22/china-beijing-cracks-down-on-unregistered-migrant-workers/.

Page 136: J.A. Mennella, "The flavor world of infants: A cross-cultural perspective" *Pediatric Basics* 77 (1996) 2-8.

Page 137–138: Background of the one-child policy: Jonathan D. Spence, *The Search for Modern China* (New York: Norton, 1990) 685-686.

249

Page 140: Conditions for women: Johnson. 2-3.

Page 142: Female infanticide: Women in World History Primary Sources. http://chnm.gmu.edu/wwh/p/59.html. Resurgence of infanticide since the one-child policy: Spence, 714.

Page 142: Chinese officials evidently agree that selective abortion is a serious problem because they have responded by making female abortion a crime and by trying to make family planning propaganda more palatable. http://www.atimes.com/atimes/China/GB08Ad02.html and http://www.independent.co.uk/news/world/asia/china-tones-down-hardline-slogans-on-onechild-policy-460457.html.

Page 142: Gender imbalance: http://english.peopledaily.com.cn/200408/25/eng20040825_154752.html, among other sources.

Page 145: Ethics: Most foundlings in China are presumed available because of the one-child policy combined with the traditional preference (or felt need) for a son, and until recently, the country's adoption process was considered one of the most corruption-proof in the world, but baby trafficking in China is not unknown. The switch from a communist to a capitalist economy means the system is increasingly driven by money. http://query.nytimes.com/gst/fullpage.html?res=9803E 5DE173DF937A15754C0A9629C8B63 and http://www.washingtonpost.com/wp-dyn/content/article/2006/03/11/AR2006031100942_pf.html.

The Hunan case is particularly troubling to the consciences of Western adoptive families because orphanage directors known to be involved in the international adoption program were buying infants from the traffickers. The China Center for Adoption Affairs conducted an investigation after the fact and claims that none of the kidnapped babies were internationally adopted, but this is small comfort to many.

In 2000, when we adopted, one reason we chose China was because we believed this kind of thing didn't happen there. Clearly, it does happen there. Brian Stuy (at research-china.blogspot.com) cites the case of a woman who, when it was discovered that she and thirty-nine other women in a small Yunnan village were getting pregnant in order to sell their children to traffickers, said: "If you want to make money, simply have a baby. Having a baby is faster than feeding a pig" (*Yunnan Legal Daily*, 7/28/04).

Page 146: John Pomfret and Deborah Nelson, "In Rural China, a Genetic Mother Lode," *Washington Post*, December 20, 2000.

Page 148: Kay Ann Johnson, Huang Banghau, and Wang Liyao, "Infant Abandonment and Adoption in China," *Population and Development Review* (September, 1998) 469.

"Push-Me-Pull-You"

Page 152: Bessel van der Kolk has proposed a new classification called Complex Developmental Trauma, which in my opinion holds greater explanatory power than any of the existing psychiatric labels. Children exposed in infancy or toddlerhood to complex trauma (such as abandonment, chronic neglect, or multiple changes of caregivers) may suffer overlapping and intertwined impairments in attachment, biological function, emotional regulation, behavioural control, dissocia-

tion, cognition, and self-concept. www.traumacenter.org/
products/ Complex%20Trauma%20White%20Paper.pdf.

Page 157: Consistent consequences or paradoxical reactions?: One
school of thought suggests that traumatized children require
immediate consequences for every instance of disobedience;
another suggests that these children frequently do best with
paradoxical reactions, for example, a hug each time they hit,
or "practising" the undesired behaviour. See, for example,
Daniel A. Hughes, *Facilitating Developmental Attachment: The
Road to Emotional Recovery and Behavioral Change in Foster and
Adopted Children* (Northvale, NJ: Jason Aronson, 1997).
Love and Logic or 1, 2, 3 Magic: Two approaches to discipline.
The first forswears "warnings" in favour of offering choices,
whereas the second suggests giving children time to comply.

"Mind Reader"

Page 169: History of phrenology: Dr. John van Wyhe, "The
History of Phrenology on the Web." http://web.archive.org/
web/20070331213827/http:/pages.britishlibrary.net/phrenol-
ogy/.

Page 169: Ambrose Bierce, *The Devil's Dictionary*. Text by
Ambrose Bierce, 1911; Etext version by Aloysius West, 1993.
http://www.alcyone.com/max/lit/devils/p.html.

"The Easy Way"

Page 177: This rosy view of transracial adoption is disputed by
many transracially adopted adults, who feel it's impossible to
compensate for the loss of identity and culture. See, for
example, Jane Jeong Trenka, Julia Chinyere Oparah and Sun
Yung Shin, Eds., *Outsiders Within: Writing on Transracial Adoption* (Cambridge, MA: South End Press, 2006).

Page 183: See Elizabeth Bartholet, *Family Bonds: Adoption, Infertility, and the New World of Child Production* (Boston: Beacon Press, 1999) 48-50.

Page 184: Charles Manson: In fact, Manson never was adopted. His mother tried to have him placed in a foster home but was unsuccessful; after she relinquished him he lived in a reform school. Vincent Bugliosi with Curt Gentry, *Helter Skelter: The True Story of the Manson Murders* (New York: Norton, 2001) 136-137.

"Mama's Voices"

For biographical details on Lana Turner I consulted www.cmgww.com/stars/turner/biography.html and www.lana turneronline.com.

Page 205: Symptoms of larynx cancer: www.ucsfhealth.org/ adult/medical_services/cancer/head_and_neck/conditions/ larynx

Page 206: Annie Dillard, "To Fashion a Text," in Zinsser, William, *Inventing the Truth: The Art and Craft of Memoir* (New York: Houghton Mifflin, 1998) 156, 161.

Page 206: Joan Didion, *Slouching Towards Bethlehem* (New York: Farrar, Straus, Giroux, 1968) Preface.

Page 210: *Laryngectomy:* Adapted from www.medicinet.com.

Page 211: Darsie Bowden, "The Rise of a Metaphor: 'Voice' in Composition Pedagogy," *Rhetoric Review* 143 (Autumn, 1995) 173. Used by permission.

Page 212: Ted Solotaroff, "Writing in the Cold," *Granta* 18 (Spring, 1985) 264-279.

Page 217: Steven Shwartz. "Finding a Voice in America," in Charles Baxter & Peter Turchi, eds, *Bringing the Devil to His Knees: The Craft of Fiction and the Writing Life* (Ann Arbor: University of Michigan Press, 2004). Used by permission of the author.

"Answering Moneta"

Page 219: Moneta, "the admonisher," was one of several names given to the Roman goddess Juno, in whose temple money was coined. Juno was primarily a goddess of women, a giver of counsel. Although she was commonly identified with the Greek goddess Hera, in "The Fall of Hyperion" Keats conflates her with Mnemosyne, or Memory, mother of the Muses.

Page 219 and following: For biographical information about Keats and his medical training, I am especially indebted to Donald Goellnicht's *The Poet Physician: Keats and Medical Science* (Pittsburgh: University of Pittsburgh Press, 1984) and to Andrew Motion's *Keats* (London: Faber and Faber, 1997).

Page 222-224: Charles Cowden Clarke, "Biographical Notes on Keats, 16 March, 1846," in Howard Edward Rollins, ed., *The Keats Circle: Letters and Papers 1816–1878, Vol. II* #187 (Cambridge, MA: Harvard University Press, 1948) 148-49.

Page 226: John Keats, "Letter to John Taylor, 27 February, 1818," in Maurice Buxton Forman, ed., *The Letters of John Keats, Vol. I* #48 (Oxford: Oxford University Press, 1931) 116.

Page 226: The term "Miltonic verse" is Keats's. "Letter to John Hamilton Reynolds, 21 September, 1819," in *The Letters of John Keats, Vol. I* #142, 419.

Page 226: Out loud and bold: John Keats, "On First Looking Into Chapman's Homer," in David Perkins, ed., *English Romantic Writers* (San Diego: Harcourt, 1967) 1126.

Page 226-229: John Keats,"The Fall of Hyperion," in *English Romantic Writers*, pages 1197-1203.

Page 230: John Taylor, "Letter to Richard Woodhouse: Memoranda of the Keats Family, 20, 23 April 1827," in *The Keats Circle*, *Vol. I*. #140, 307.

Page 230-231: John Keats. "Letter to Richard Woodhouse, 27 October, 1818" in *The Letters of John Keats, Vol. I* #88, 245.

Page 231: Paul Fussell, *Poetic Meter and Poetic Form* (New York: Random House, 1979) 57-59.

Page 232: Motion, 10.

Page 233: Keats, "The Fall of Hyperion," *English Romantic Writers*, 1201.

Page 233: Keats, "Ode to a Nightingale," *English Romantic Writers*, 1184.

Page 234: Nothing ever becomes real till it is experienced. Keats, "Letter to George and Georgiana Keats, February 14-May 3, 1819," *The Letters of John Keats, Vol. II* #114, 342.

Page 234: Information on body-snatchers: Donald C. Goellnicht, *The Poet-Physician: Keats and Medical Science* (University of Pittsburgh Press, 1984) 29.

Page 236: Charles Armitage Brown, "Life of John Keats, 19 March 1841," Rollins, Ed. *The Keats Circle: Letters and Papers 1816-1878, Vol. II. #166*, 73.

Page 236: John Keats, "Letter to Charles Brown, 30 November, 1820," *The Letters of John Keats, Vol. II.* #227, 571-572. This is Keats's final letter. He ends, 'I can scarcely bid you good-bye, even in a letter. I always made an awkward bow."

Page 236: Joseph Severn, "Letter to John Taylor, 6 March 1821" in *The Keats Circle, Vol. I.* #107, 224.

Acknowledgements

Thanks, first, to my editor, Melanie Little, whose faith in this book renewed my own and whose perceptive suggestions made it immeasurably stronger. No writer could ask for a more generous or discerning reader, and I'm enormously in her debt. Thanks also to Peter Norman for his sensitive and thoughtful copy edits.

Portions of this book appeared in a somewhat different form in the following publications:

"Pathology" in *Event* 26.3. The essay was also broadcast on CKLN Radio, Toronto, excerpted in *The Totally Unknown Writers Festival Stories* (Life Rattle New Writers Series), and featured in the CBC OUTFRONT documentary "Unknown Writers." "The Other Country" in *Under the Sun* (Cookeville, TN), and in *Body Breakdowns: Tales of Illness and Recovery*, edited by Janis Harper (Anvil Press). "On Separation" in *Prairie Fire* 27.2. "Walls of Glass" in *Prairie Fire* 19.4; excerpts also appeared as "Soldier Boy" in *The Use of Personal Narratives in the Helping Professions*, edited by Jessica Heriot and Eileen Polinger (The Haworth Press). Parts of "How to Be a Volunteer" appeared as "A Chain of Being" in

Event 30.1, and other parts as the short story "Love, Belonging" in *The Windsor Review* 36.1. "Female Troubles" in *River Teeth: A Journal of Nonfiction Narrative* 2.1. "At Lingyin Si" in *Event* 33.3 and in *The Lucky Ones: Our Stories of Adopting Children from China*, edited by Ann Rauhala (ECW Press). "Push-Me-Pull-You" in *Prairie Fire* 26.2. "The Easy Way" in *Between Interruptions: Mothers Write on Guilt, Anxiety, Ambition, and More*, edited by Cori Howard (Key Porter Books). "Mama's Voices" in *The New Quarterly* 103, and in *Double Lives: Writing and Motherhood*, edited by Shannon Cowan, Fiona Tinwei Lam and Cathy Stonehouse (McGill-Queen's University Press). "Answering Moneta" in *Water~Stone* 3.1.

Thanks to the editors of these journals and anthologies, and especially to Calvin Wharton and Billeh Nickerson at *Event*; Andris Taskans, Heidi Harms, and Janine Tarnopolsky at *Prairie Fire*; and Kim Jernigan at *The New Quarterly*. Their ongoing encouragement lightened the days.

I'm grateful for financial support at various times from The Canada Council for the Arts and the Ontario Arts Council, from the University of British Columbia and Middlebury College, and most of all, from my family.

I wrote some of the manuscript at UBC's Department of Creative Writing. Thanks to Lynne Bowen, George McWhirter, and Don Mowatt—exemplary models; to Linda Svendsen and Rhea Tregebov—encouraging spirits; and especially to Keith Maillard and Andreas Schroeder, who always seemed to know when to nudge and when to step aside, and whose belief in this book was unwavering.

I've been blessed with many writer friends who read the manuscript in whole or in part over the years and offered helpful suggestions or encouragement. Thanks to: Paul Austin, Walter Bennett, Diana Fitzgerald Bryden, Xujun Eberlein, Tom Elliott, Stephen Gauer, Kathy Diane Leveille, Jim Paul, and Phyllis Vine. The members of the THC brightened many a Vancouver breakfast: Terry Dove, Carla Gillis, Sarah Leavitt, Joe Wiebe, and Robert Weston. Judy McFarlane, Rachel Rose, and Jane Silcott inspired me with their own words and renewed my commitment. Fiona Tinwei Lam listened and urged me to write my heart's truth. And Kelly Cooper gave the gift of time and her always empathetic attention. Thanks to all—companions in the craft.

I'm grateful for the online support I received from fellow adoptive parents—too many to name—and for professional help from Suki Falkner, Brenda Knight, Brenda Pulvermacher, and Paul and Mari Swingle as well as for childcare from Susan Hawkins. Michael and Toni Pickard provided a comfortable hideaway and a warm fire during the final phases of editing. Thanks also to Donna Katinas, Danielle Michel, Susan Fisher, and Heather Shaw for sustaining friendship, and to Shayna Watson, who is every writer's dream—a genuine, disinterested reader.

Most of all, I would like to thank my family. Joshua, Noah, and Zipporah Weisberg welcomed me graciously into their lives and continue to put up with my cooking.

My brother, Mark, provides a living example of a stead-fast heart. My husband, Mark Weisberg, is my first reader and trusted friend. His love and support make it possible for me to write and his encouragement released the words. This book would not exist without him.

I owe a very special debt to my daughter, Maia. Knowing that I'd written about the challenges we've faced together, she chose to be called by her real name in these essays. As someone who often asks me to tell her a "non-fiction" story about my own life, she intuitively grasps the healing properties of true stories. At eight she is a strong, increasingly resilient, and loving girl, whose creative adaptations will one day delight the world as they consistently delight me.

Finally, I want to thank my parents. The depth of their love and support may be more evident to me now that I'm a parent myself, but their fortitude was never in question. I hope their courage, humour, and compassion inform this book. Its flaws are of course my own, but its strengths I owe largely to their example.

Susan Olding was recently named one of *The New Quarterly*'s "Most Loved Living Writers" alongside authors including Patrick Lane and Alice Munro. Her poetry and prose have appeared widely in literary journals and anthologies across Canada and the United States. She has been a finalist for a National Magazine Award, two Western Magazine Awards, and a CBC Literary Award; she is also a two-time winner of the *Event* Creative Non-fiction Contest, as well as winner of the *Prairie Fire* Non-fiction Contest and the Brenda Ueland Prose Prize for Literary Non-fiction.

Born in Toronto, Susan Olding currently lives with her family in Kingston, Ontario, where she works at the Queen's University Writing Centre.